Teen Pregnancy and Parenting

Other Books in the Current Controversies Series:

Teen Pregnancy and Parenting

Helen Cothran, *Book Editor*

David Bender, *Publisher*
Bruno Leone, *Executive Editor*

Bonnie Szumski, *Editorial Director*
Stuart B. Miller, *Managing Editor*

CURRENT CONTROVERSIES

Cover photo: © David Young-Wolff/PhotoEdit

Library of Congress Cataloging-in-Publication Data

Teen pregnancy and parenting / Helen Cothran, book editor.
        p. cm. — (Current controversies)
    Includes bibliographical references and index.
    ISBN 0-7377-0557-4 (pbk. : alk. paper) — ISBN 0-7377-0558-2
(lib. bdg. : alk. paper)
    1. Teenage pregnancy—United States. 2. Teenage mothers—United
States. I. Cothran, Helen. II. Series.

HQ759.4 .T422 2001
306.874'3—dc21   00-058714
                                                                        CIP

©2001 by Greenhaven Press, Inc., PO Box 289009, San Diego, CA 92198-9009
Printed in the U.S.A.

Contents

Chapter 1: Is Teenage Pregnancy a Serious Problem?

Yes: Teenage Pregnancy Is a Serious Problem

No: Teenage Pregnancy Is Not a Serious Problem

who are born out of wedlock, the majority of pregnancies that end in abortion each year, and for the contraction of most sexually transmitted diseases.

Chapter 2: What Factors Contribute to Teenage Pregnancy?

Chapter 3: How Can Teenage Pregnancy Be Prevented?

higher rates of transmission of sexually transmitted diseases. Teenagers need to be taught to wait to have sex until marriage if they want to experience lasting intimate relationships and more satisfying sex.

Chapter 4: What Alternatives to Parenting Exist for Pregnant Teens?

Chapter 5: Should Society Approve of Teenage Parenting?

Foreword

By definition, controversies are "discussions of questions in which opposing opinions clash" (Webster's Twentieth Century Dictionary Unabridged). Few would deny that controversies are a pervasive part of the human condition and exist on virtually every level of human enterprise. Controversies transpire between individuals and among groups, within nations and between nations. Controversies supply the grist necessary for progress by providing challenges and challengers to the status quo. They also create atmospheres where strife and warfare can flourish. A world without controversies would be a peaceful world; but it also would be, by and large, static and prosaic.

The Series' Purpose

The purpose of the Current Controversies series is to explore many of the social, political, and economic controversies dominating the national and international scenes today. Titles selected for inclusion in the series are highly focused and specific. For example, from the larger category of criminal justice, Current Controversies deals with specific topics such as police brutality, gun control, white collar crime, and others. The debates in Current Controversies also are presented in a useful, timeless fashion. Articles and book excerpts included in each title are selected if they contribute valuable, long-range ideas to the overall debate. And wherever possible, current information is enhanced with historical documents and other relevant materials. Thus, while individual titles are current in focus, every effort is made to ensure that they will not become quickly outdated. Books in the Current Controversies series will remain important resources for librarians, teachers, and students for many years.

In addition to keeping the titles focused and specific, great care is taken in the editorial format of each book in the series. Book introductions and chapter prefaces are offered to provide background material for readers. Chapters are organized around several key questions that are answered with diverse opinions representing all points on the political spectrum. Materials in each chapter include opinions in which authors clearly disagree as well as alternative opinions in which authors may agree on a broader issue but disagree on the possible solutions. In this way, the content of each volume in Current Controversies mirrors the mosaic of opinions encountered in society. Readers will quickly realize that there are many viable answers to these complex issues. By questioning each author's conclusions, students and casual readers can begin to develop the critical thinking skills so important to evaluating opinionated material.

Current Controversies is also ideal for controlled research. Each anthology in the series is composed of primary sources taken from a wide gamut of informational categories including periodicals, newspapers, books, United States and foreign government documents, and the publications of private and public organizations. Readers will find factual support for reports, debates, and research papers covering all areas of important issues. In addition, an annotated table of contents, an index, a book and periodical bibliography, and a list of organizations to contact are included in each book to expedite further research.

Perhaps more than ever before in history, people are confronted with diverse and contradictory information. During the Persian Gulf War, for example, the public was not only treated to minute-to-minute coverage of the war, it was also inundated with critiques of the coverage and countless analyses of the factors motivating U.S. involvement. Being able to sort through the plethora of opinions accompanying today's major issues, and to draw one's own conclusions, can be a complicated and frustrating struggle. It is the editors' hope that Current Controversies will help readers with this struggle.

Greenhaven Press anthologies primarily consist of previously published material taken from a variety of sources, including periodicals, books, scholarly journals, newspapers, government documents, and position papers from private and public organizations. These original sources are often edited for length and to ensure their accessibility for a young adult audience. The anthology editors also change the original titles of these works in order to clearly present the main thesis of each viewpoint and to explicitly indicate the opinion presented in the viewpoint. These alterations are made in consideration of both the reading and comprehension levels of a young adult audience. Every effort is made to ensure that Greenhaven Press accurately reflects the original intent of the authors included in this anthology.

Introduction

The teen birthrate in the United States is the highest of any industrialized nation. According to the Robin Hood Foundation, an organization that works to improve the lives of impoverished children, "each year, nearly one million teenagers in the United States—approximately 10 percent of all fifteen- to nineteen-year-old females—become pregnant." Over half of pregnant teens (more than a half million teens) give birth, and the vast majority of teens who bear children—72 percent—are unmarried. The Robin Hood Foundation reports that "more than 80 percent of these young mothers end up in poverty and reliant on welfare." In addition, the children of teen mothers suffer more problems than the children of older parents. The Robin Hood Foundation reports that the children of adolescent mothers tend to have lower birth weights, have more childhood health problems, suffer more abuse and neglect, have more trouble in school, and grow up without fathers. Moreover, daughters of teen mothers are more likely to become teen mothers themselves, and the sons of unwed teen mothers are more likely than their peers to wind up in prison.

In response to the high rates of teen pregnancy and the social and economic problems that many experts associate with it, countless strategies have been tried to reduce adolescent pregnancy and childbearing. Many of these approaches are educational. For example, some schools provide abstinence-based sex education while others distribute condoms and offer guidance on how to use them. Other approaches to reducing teen pregnancy are social: Some state governments finance homes for pregnant teens, for example, and provide free health services to adolescents. Some approaches to preventing teenage pregnancy are punitive, such as denying welfare benefits to pregnant teens or enforcing statutory rape laws. One such punitive approach is the enforcement of fornication laws.

About one-third of all states have laws that prohibit fornication, which is defined as sex between unmarried people of the opposite sex. Most of these laws date back to the early part of the twentieth century or earlier and have largely been ignored. But in some areas of the country—such as in the town of Emmett in Gem County, Idaho—prosecutors have begun to enforce fornication laws in an effort to stem teenage pregnancy rates. When the teen mothers apply for welfare, city and county attorneys are given their names—and whenever possible, those of the fathers—to prosecute. Those convicted of fornication must pay a fine of up to $300 and spend up to six months in jail.

Introduction

Advocates of fornication law enforcement argue that such a punitive approach will send a message to other teens and adult males who impregnate teen girls that there are legal consequences to engaging in risky sexual behavior. Douglas Varie, the attorney who first dusted off the fornication law in Emmett, hopes that enforcing the law will prohibit many teens from having sex and will force boys to be financially responsible for their children. He contends, "children having children imposes a heavy burden on society." He also wants to "do everything possible to ensure that [teen fathers] have contact with the child. It's a sad thing for a child to only know his or her natural father as someone who had a good time with his mother in the back seat of a car."

Many are critical of fornication law enforcement, however. Critics like Robin Abcarian, co-host of a morning talk show in Los Angeles, wonder how after-the-fact prosecutions can help teenagers. She asks: "Wouldn't it make better sense, and accomplish more, to put our money and energy into sex education and contraception?" Critics of the law assert that sex education is necessary because many adolescents are uninformed about the possible adverse consequences of sexual activity. Jeanette Germain of Planned Parenthood laments, "we have the highest teen pregnancy rate in the developed world because we don't educate our teens." While Germain does not support enforcement of fornication laws as the solution to teen pregnancy, she has seen one positive result in Gem County: More families who live in Emmett are driving to sex education classes offered by Planned Parenthood in Boise.

Other opponents contend that enforcement is unfair. Amanda Smisek, a Gem County teen who was prosecuted for fornication, asserts, "What makes me mad is that if they're going to charge people with fornication, they should charge it equally—to adults, too—and they don't do that." Smisek and her boyfriend pleaded not guilty, with the support of her mother, to the fornication charges. Although their cases generated public sympathy, both teens were convicted. Neither had to go to jail or pay fines, but they were required to attend parenting classes together, complete their high school education, stay employed, and stay off drugs, alcohol, and cigarettes.

The American Civil Liberties Union (ACLU) agreed that the enforcement of fornication charges against Smisek violated constitutional equal-protection guarantees. The ACLU also argued that the government was not acting in the best interest of its citizens. Jack Van Valkenburgh of the ACLU contends that "prosecuting a 17-year-old for fornication, over her mother's objections, represents the worst kind of government interference in the family." Because the Idaho teens were prosecuted only after they applied for state assistance, moreover, many critics worry that the government is unfairly targeting the poor in order to reduce public spending. Kristin Luker, author of *Dubious Conceptions*, a book about teenage pregnancy, warns of "the symbolic use of these archaic laws to demonize and punish the poor."

Few states prosecute teenagers for fornication, but many are watching the

Emmett experiment to see if it works to curb teen pregnancy. Although the rates of teenage pregnancy have decreased slightly since 1992, the public's concern about the consequences of early childbearing have not abated. While some experts argue that education and social services are the best way to address teen pregnancy, others contend that punitive approaches are most effective. The authors in *Teen Pregnancy and Parenting: Current Controversies* discuss whether or not teen pregnancy is a serious problem, the factors that contribute to teen pregnancy, what alternatives exist to teen parenting, and the approaches that society should take to address the issue.

Chapter 1

Is Teenage Pregnancy a Serious Problem?

CURRENT CONTROVERSIES

Chapter Preface

The teen birth rate has been dropping steadily during the last ten years. In 1999, the *New York Times* reported that "births to teens ages 15 to 19 dropped by 2 percent from 1997. They dropped 18 percent from 1991 through 1998." The newspaper also reported that births to girls ages 10 to 14 were the lowest since 1969. Despite decreasing teen pregnancy rates, however, the issue of teen pregnancy continues to be a focal point in political campaigns and the subject of media attention: Politicians, columnists, educators, researchers, and others seem to argue unceasingly about the extent of the problem. Some assert that teen pregnancy is society's most serious issue, while others contend that the problem has been overstated.

Those who believe that teen pregnancy is a serious problem argue that teenage pregnancy causes a number of serious social ills. They contend that teen parents are less likely to continue their education and more likely to live in poverty than their childless peers. Many commentators argue that children born to teens have more problems than other children and often become teen parents themselves. Columnist Suzanne Fields maintains that "increasing numbers of children born to children are likely to repeat the devastating cycles of almost everything bad—teen-age pregnancy, school failure, early behavioral problems, drug abuse, child abuse, depression and crime." These problems, she maintains, are exacerbated by the high rates of teenage childbearing. Kathleen Sylvester of the Progressive Policy Institute claims that "each year, more than one million American teenage girls become pregnant—one in nine . . . [and] about half of these young women give birth."

Others argue that politicians and the media have exaggerated the extent of the teen pregnancy problem. They maintain that politicians use the issue of teen pregnancy to play on society's fears and win public support for their campaigns. But their arguments are based on assumptions about teen pregnancy that are not true, dissenters argue. Most of the social ills that conservatives attribute to teenage childbearing, for example, are actually caused by poverty, they assert. Janine Jackson, research director for *EXTRA!* magazine, contends that "substantial evidence shows that while single motherhood is associated with poverty, it does not *cause* poverty." She asserts that teenagers who get pregnant were already living at or below the poverty line. Furthermore, many critics contend that early childbearing can actually improve some teens' lives. Mike Males, author of *The Scapegoat Generation*, argues that teen girls who are living in less than ideal circumstances may be exercising their best option when they decide to become mothers. Males notes that teens often escape the impoverished and abusive households in which they were raised when they become pregnant by older men who have the resources to help them.

In spite of the fact that teen pregnancy rates are declining, people still argue vociferously about the extent of the teen pregnancy problem. Many contend that teen pregnancy causes many of society's most entrenched problems while others maintain that teen pregnancy is a symptom of those problems. The authors in the following chapter present a variety of viewpoints about the seriousness of the teen pregnancy problem.

Teen Pregnancy Is a Serious Problem

by National Campaign to Prevent Teen Pregnancy

About the author: *The National Campaign to Prevent Teen Pregnancy is a nonprofit organization that supports a pregnancy-free adolescence.*

Teenage childbearing is associated with adverse consequences for teenage mothers and particularly for their children. However, most of the negative consequences for teen mothers—some say all—are due to the disadvantaged situations in which many of these girls already live. In other words, it is not as if all teen mothers were doing well *before* giving birth and then sank into poverty and social disorganization only as a result of having a child. Researchers are continuing to sort out the extent to which poor outcomes for teen mothers are due to the timing of the birth versus characteristics of the mother that were present even before she became pregnant. However, most experts agree that, although the disadvantaged backgrounds of most teen mothers account for many of the burdens that these young women shoulder, having a baby during adolescence only makes matters worse.

The Adverse Consequences of Teen Pregnancy

Thus, when compared to similarly situated women who delay childbearing until age 20 or 21, adolescent mothers and their children experience a number of adverse social and economic consequences. For instance, early parenting limits a young mother's likelihood of completing the high school and postsecondary education necessary to qualify for a well-paying job. Less than one-third of teens who begin their families before age 18 ever complete high school. If they delay childbearing until age 20 or 21, the odds of high school graduation for these young mothers increases to 50 percent (Figure 1).

Teen mothers spend more of their young adult years as single parents than do women who delay childbearing, which means that their children spend much of their young lives with only one parent. Children who grow up in single-parent homes are disadvantaged in many ways. For example, when compared with

Excerpted with permission from "Whatever Happened to Childhood? The Problem of Teen Pregnancy in the United States," by The National Campaign to Prevent Teen Pregnancy, May 1997.

similarly situated children who grow up with two parents, children in one-parent families are twice as likely to drop out of high school, 2.5 times as likely to become teen mothers, and 1.4 times as likely to be both out of school and out of work. Even after adjusting for a variety of relevant social and economic differences, children in single-parent homes have lower grade point averages, lower college aspirations, and poorer school attendance records. As adults, they have higher rates of divorce.

Figure 1. Teen mothers are less likely to complete high school

Teenage Mothers:
Educational Attainment by Age 30

☐ High School
   Diploma

■ No High School
   Diploma

32%

Mothers Who Delay Childbearing Until
Age 20 or 21: Estimated Educational
Attainment by Age 30

☐ High School
   Diploma

■ No High School
   Diploma

50%

Adolescent mothers also have more children, on average, than women who delay childbearing, which makes it more difficult for them and their children to escape a life of poverty. About one-fourth of teenage mothers have a second child within 24 months of the first birth; this percentage is even higher for younger teen mothers than for older ones. As a result, adolescent mothers must stretch their limited incomes to support more children.

Many young mothers end up on welfare (Figure 2). Data show that almost half of all teenage mothers and over three-fourths of *unmarried* teen mothers began receiving Aid to Families with Dependent Children (AFDC) within five years of

Figure 2. Many teen mothers end up on welfare, especially if they are unmarried

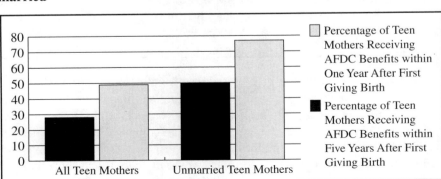

☐ Percentage of Teen Mothers Receiving AFDC Benefits within One Year After First Giving Birth

■ Percentage of Teen Mothers Receiving AFDC Benefits within Five Years After First Giving Birth

the birth of their first child. In addition, 52 percent of *all* mothers on AFDC had their first child as a teenager.

Conversely, the fathers of children born to teenage mothers bear relatively little of the measurable costs of adolescent childbearing, although anecdotal evidence suggests some fathers bear emotional or other costs that have not been well-studied. Nearly 80 percent of these fathers do not marry the young mothers of their first children, and, on average, these absent fathers pay less than $800 annually for child support. Otherwise, the measurable effects for the fathers are limited to somewhat lower education levels and to modest earnings losses—on the order of 10 to 15 percent annually.

The Children of Teens Suffer Most

By far , the greatest harm is borne by the children of teen mothers. In fact, the difficulties experienced by these children begin before birth and continue into adulthood. For example, the children of teen mothers (particularly mothers under 18) are more likely to be born prematurely and at low birthweight (Figure 3). Low birthweight (less than five-and-a-half pounds) raises the probabilities of infant death, blindness, deafness, chronic respiratory problems, mental retardation, mental illness, and cerebral palsy. In addition, low birthweight doubles the chance that a child will later be diagnosed as having dyslexia, hyperactivity, or another disability.

Figure 3. The children of teen mothers have lower birthweights

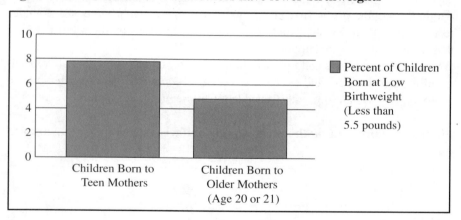

Despite having more health problems than the children of older mothers, the children of teen mothers receive less medical care and treatment. In his or her first 14 years, the average child of a teen mother visits a physician or other medical provider an average of 3.8 times per year, compared with 4.3 times per year for the children of later childbearers.

Children of teen mothers also do much worse in school than those born to older parents. They are 50 percent more likely to repeat a grade, they perform much worse on standardized tests of performance, and ultimately they are less likely to complete high school than if their mothers had delayed childbearing (Figure 4).

Figure 4. The children of teen mothers have poorer school performance

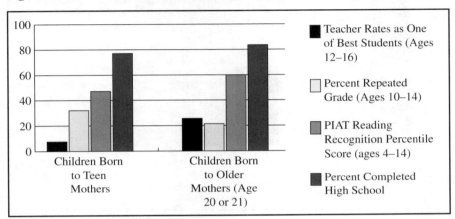

Children born to teen mothers are also at higher risk because their mothers—and often their fathers as well—are typically too young to master the demanding job of being parents. Still growing and developing themselves, teen mothers are often unable to provide the kind of environment that infants and very young children require for optimal development. Recent research, for example, has clarified the critical importance of early cognitive stimulation for adequate brain development.

Abuse and Neglect

Measured against national norms, the children of adolescent parents live in homes that are of poorer overall quality (e.g. poorer physical conditions, less parent-child interaction, and fewer educationally stimulating resources in the home). These limitations are reflected in poorer academic performance by the children, less attention given to their health problems, and higher rates of behavior problems.

> *"When compared to similarly situated women who delay childbearing . . . , adolescent mothers and their children experience a number of adverse . . . consequences."*

The children of teen parents also suffer higher rates of abuse and neglect than would occur if their mothers had delayed childbearing (Figure 5). There are 110 reported incidents of abuse and neglect per 1,000 families headed by a young teen mother. If mothers delay childbearing until their early twenties, the rate drops by half—to 51 incidents per 1,000 families. Similarly,

Figure 5. The children of teen mothers are at greater risk of abuse and neglect

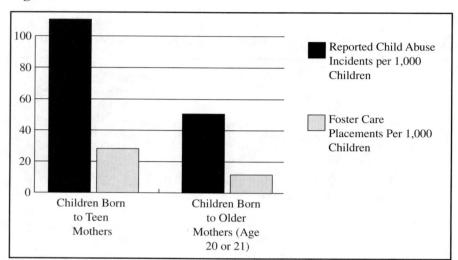

rates of foster care placement are significantly higher for children whose mothers are under 18. In fact, over half of foster care placements of children with young mothers could be averted simply by delaying childbearing a few years, thereby saving taxpayers nearly $1 billion annually in foster care costs alone.

Adolescent childbearing contributes to the high rates of economic inactivity among young adults and of crime among young men, as well as to a repetitive cycle of teen parenting. Young adult children of teen mothers are 30 percent more likely to be neither working nor going to school. The sons of teen mothers are 13 percent more likely to end up in prison. And, the teen daughters are 22 percent more likely to become teen mothers themselves.

Taxpayers pay a high price for teen childbearing. A recent study found that, after controlling for differences between teen mothers and mothers aged 20 or 21 when they had their first child, teen childbearing costs taxpayers $6.9 billion each year—$2,831 a year per teen mother (Figure 6). . . .

The Basic Messages

Most fundamentally, the nation needs to embrace the basic social norm that the teenage years are for education and growing up, not pregnancy and parenthood. One of the reasons the United States has such high levels of teen pregnancy and childbearing is that the consensus that "teen pregnancy is not OK" is less robust than many imagine. There has been a sea change in attitudes and behavior over the past few decades with the result that teen sexual activity and out-of-wedlock births are now commonplace. Partly as a result, not all young people—and not even all adults—place a high priority on avoiding teen preg-

Figure 6. Taxpayers pay a high price for teen childbearing (estimated annual costs to taxpayers of teen childbearing, 1996 dollars)

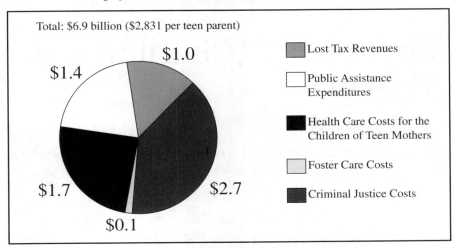

nancy. When asked why they became pregnant, many teenage girls respond, "it just sort of happened," a response that is consistent with research showing clearly that unless motivation is strong to avoid pregnancy, it can happen all too easily. Adults need to speak directly to teens about this issue, providing guidance in accordance with their own values and encouraging teens to make much clearer choices about when to become sexually active and how to handle the responsibilities that such a decision entails.

In communicating this basic message, the consequences of teen pregnancy should be emphasized. As the data summarized above show, teen pregnancy and childbearing impose significant costs, both economic and personal, and place major burdens on families and communities. Teenage pregnancy and childbearing are not in anyone's best interest, least of all the children born to teenage mothers. Keeping these consequences squarely before the public can help motivate both adolescents and adults to take action to reduce teen pregnancy.

Illegitimacy Contributes to Poverty

by Isabel V. Sawhill

About the author: *Isabel V. Sawhill is president of the National Campaign to Prevent Teen Pregnancy and a senior fellow at the Brookings Institute, a private research and education organization.*

I appreciate the opportunity to testify on this important topic. Both as President of the National Campaign to Prevent Teen Pregnancy and as a Senior Fellow at the Brookings Institution, I have become convinced that early out-of-wedlock childbearing is bad for parents, bad for society, and especially bad for the children born into such families. However, the views I express today are my own and should not be attributed to a particular institution with which I am associated.

Out-of-Wedlock Childbearing Causes Poverty

Three years after the enactment of welfare reform in 1996, the new law is being hailed as a great success. Caseloads have declined dramatically since the law was signed, and with fewer individuals to support, the states are flush with money. A strong economy interacting with tougher welfare rules and more support for the working poor is helping to turn welfare checks into paychecks. But the welfare system is like a revolving door. In good times, more people move off the rolls than come on and caseloads decline. But in bad times, exactly the reverse can occur. The only way to permanently reduce poverty and its associated expense is to stem the longer-term trends in out-of-wedlock childbearing that have historically pushed child poverty and caseloads up. Unless the states invest their surplus funds in programs aimed at preventing poverty, success may be short-lived or purchased at the expense of the children it was designed to help. If every recipient who finds a job is replaced by a younger sister ill-prepared to support a family, the immutability of the revolving door will once again prevail.

There are many ways of preventing poverty. We could invest in early childhood education, inner city schools, or in additional supports for the working

Testimony given by Isabel V. Sawhill before the Subcommittee on Human Resources, Committee on Ways and Means, June 29, 1999, Washington, D.C.

poor. But unless we can reduce out-of-wedlock pregnancies and encourage the formation of two-parent families, other efforts, by themselves, may well fail.

Much more attention needs to be given to encouraging young people to defer childbearing until they are ready to be parents. Some of the funds freed up by the drop in caseloads ought to be invested in teen pregnancy prevention programs and in reconnecting fathers with their children. In the absence of such efforts, welfare reform's current success is likely to be short-lived.

Family Structure and Welfare Dependency

Rising divorce rates combined with a huge increase in childbearing outside of marriage have led to a situation in which most children born today will spend some time in a single-parent family. And since roughly half of these single parents are poor, large numbers of children are growing up in poverty as well. Indeed, the growth of single-parent families can account for virtually all of the increase in child poverty since 1970.

The growth of female-headed families has also contributed to the growth of the welfare rolls. According to the Congressional Budget Office, welfare caseloads would have declined considerably throughout most of the 1980s if it had not been for the fact that the growth of single-parent families continued to push them upwards. Moreover, this factor was more than twice as important as the economy in accounting for the roughly one million increase in the basic caseload between 1989 and 1993.

> *"The only way to permanently reduce poverty and its associated expense is to stem the longer-term trends in out-of-wedlock childbearing."*

It is not just the growth of female-headed families but also shifts in the composition of the group that have contributed to greater poverty and welfare dependency. In the 1960s and 1970s, most of the growth of single-parent families was caused by increases in divorce or separation. In the 1980s and 1990s, all of the increase has been driven by out-of-wedlock childbearing. Currently, 32 percent of all children in the United States and more than half in many large cities are born outside of marriage. Unmarried mothers tend to be younger and more disadvantaged than their divorced counterparts. They are overwhelmingly poor and about three-quarters of them end up on welfare.

A large fraction of babies born outside of marriage have mothers who are not teenagers. However, the pattern of out-of-wedlock childbearing is often established at a young age. Specifically, more than half of out-of-wedlock births are to teens. So if we want to reduce such births and the welfare dependency that usually ensues, the adolescent years are a good place to start.

There are two strategies that can be used to reduce teen, out-of-wedlock births. One is to encourage marriage. The other is to discourage sex, pregnancy, and births among teens. This latter strategy has the advantage of being more consistent with the growing requirements of the economy for workers with higher levels of education and with evidence that teenage marriages are highly unstable.

The Causes and Symptoms of Poverty

Some contend that many of the women who have babies as unmarried teens would have ended up poor and on welfare even if they had married and delayed childbearing. The argument is that they come from disadvantaged families and neighborhoods, have gone to poor schools, or faced other adverse influences that make having a baby at a young age as good an option as any other. There are few men with jobs for them to marry, and given their own lack of skills, welfare seems like a relatively good alternative. Moreover, earnings for less skilled men have plummeted over the past 30 years.

Although such arguments cannot be dismissed entirely, they are only a small part of the story. To begin with, the drop in marriage rates, which has been especially pronounced among African Americans, has been much larger than any economic model can explain. Second, early childbearers are much less likely to complete high school, leading directly to poor long-term employment prospects for the young women involved. The children in such families suffer even greater adverse consequences, including poorer health, less success in school, and more behavior problems. Finally, the argument that declining earnings has made marriage less viable is a curious one. Two adults can live more cheaply than one, and by pooling whatever earnings can be secured from even intermittent or low-paid employment, they will be better off than a single adult living alone. These arguments are doubly true once a child enters the picture and one parent either needs to stay home or shoulder the extra expense of paying for child care.

One can grant that the earnings prospects of poorly educated, inner city residents are not good and have deteriorated in recent decades, and that better schools and more support systems for low-income working families would help. Still, early out-of-wedlock childbearing greatly compounds the problem. Even well-educated individuals in their twenties have difficulty living on one income these days, and most middle class families have two earners. Yet, for some reason, it is assumed that if the men in low-income communities can't command a decent wage, they are not marriageable. But fathers are, or should be, more than a meal ticket. And although two minimum-wage jobs will not make anyone rich, they will provide an income of about $20,000 a year, well above the poverty level for a family with two children. In short, marriage and delayed childbearing have the potential to solve a lot of problems, including assuring a better future for the next generation.

> *"The growth of single-parent families can account for virtually all of the increase in child poverty since 1970."*

Why Teen Pregnancy Rates Are So High

As teen pregnancy and childbearing have become more common, they have also become more acceptable, or at least less stigmatized. A few decades ago, there were real social penalties to be paid if a girl became pregnant outside of marriage. Young girls refrained from sex for fear of becoming pregnant and being socially ostracized. Among those who did get pregnant, shotgun marriages were common. Young men had to compete for women's affections by promising marriage or at least commitment. All of this changed during the 1970s and 1980s. Contraception and abortion became much more available, women became more liberated, and sex mores changed dramatically. A study by George Akerlof and Janet Yellen documents how the decline in shotgun marriages contributed to a rising tide of out-of-wedlock births. But this same change in sexual mores led not just to fewer marriages but also to a lot more sexual activity and a rising pregnancy rate among the nation's youth.

> *"Early childbearers are less likely to complete high school, leading directly to poor long-term employment prospects for the young women involved."*

Teen pregnancy rates increased from the early 1970s until 1990 and have been declining since that time. The relatively modest growth is the result of two offsetting trends since 1972: increased sexual activity among teens combined with greater use of contraception. If teens had not increased their use of contraception over this period, teen pregnancy rates would have soared and been almost 40 percent higher by now. On the other hand, contraceptive use did not keep pace with the greater tendency of teens to engage in sex, with the result that, up until recently, the pregnancy rate kept rising. In the war between sex and safer sex, sex won. These increases in pregnancy rates have not always translated into higher birth rates. The greater availability of abortion after 1973 kept the teen birthrate somewhat in check. But few people, whatever their position on this difficult issue, want abortion to be the major means of preventing poverty and welfare dependency.

Teen Pregnancy and Birth Rates Are Now Declining

In the 1990s, teenage sexual activity stopped increasing or even declined a bit. This combined with greater utilization of contraception among teens has caused the teen pregnancy rate to decline for the first time in decades. Teen births have fallen as well and the proportion of all children born out-of-wedlock has stabilized. The drop in birth rates among unmarried black teens is especially striking. It has declined by almost one-fifth since 1991, a much sharper drop than that experienced by any other group.

What has caused this recent turnaround in sexual activity, pregnancy, and out-of-wedlock births? No one really knows but there are several possible explanations. One is fear of AIDS, which is widely suspected to be the most important reason for teens' willingness to either abstain from sex or use contraception more frequently than in the past.

Another possible explanation is welfare reform itself. Although the trends predate welfare reform, they may have gotten an extra push from the debate leading up to enactment of the new law in 1996 and the state reforms that preceded it. Most researchers don't expect welfare reform to have a big impact on out-of-wedlock childbearing. (Past studies are somewhat inconsistent, but most find that welfare has had only minor effects.) However, the new law makes welfare, and thus unwed motherhood, as a life choice much more difficult. And past research may not be a very good guide to future behavior because it has been based on variations in welfare benefits across states, not system-wide changes that are accompanied by . . . strong moral messages that have the potential to change community norms.

Another factor that can't be dismissed is the performance of the economy over this period. The unemployment rate peaked in 1992 at 7.5 percent and has fallen sharply since. The long and very robust expansion, combined with increases in the minimum wage and in the Earned Income Tax Credit (EITC), may have helped to make work more attractive than welfare, and provided young women with more of a reason to defer childbearing. (This explanation is consistent with a surprisingly steep rise in the labor force participation of less educated single mothers since 1990.) And finally, tougher enforcement of child support laws may have made young men think twice before producing a baby.

Teenage Pregnancy Rates Are Still High

Although recent declines auger well for the future, it is worth remembering that teenage pregnancy rates are still at least twice as high as in other industrialized countries and higher than they were in the early 1970s. About half of these pregnancies are carried to term while the remainder either end with a miscarriage or are terminated by an abortion. Very few teen mothers put their babies up for adoption, or marry the baby's father, a marked departure from practices 30 or 40 years ago.

All of these considerations suggest that unless welfare reform begins to modify the underlying demographic trends that contribute to poverty and welfare dependency, it may do little more than reshuffle poor mothers and their children between welfare and

"Change in sexual mores led not just to fewer marriages but also to a lot more sexual activity and a rising pregnancy rate among the nation's youth."

low-paid work or worse. With the help of a strong economy, states could end up being quite successful at moving existing recipients off the welfare rolls. But unless they also focus on the number coming in the front door of the welfare system, this could be a hollow victory. Congress has created an incentive for states to reduce teen and out-of-wedlock childbearing by offering a bonus of

$20 million annually to the most successful states, and this has served as a wake-up call for some governors. But as Richard Nathan at the State University of New York (SUNY) at Albany reports, many states have been reluctant to address the issue, considering it too hot to handle. They have tossed this political hot potato to local governments and nonprofit organizations.

Solutions

Efforts to reduce teen pregnancy have traditionally centered on sex education and family planning services. Sex education, although widely available, is often too little and too late to have much impact. The best curricula focus less on reproductive biology than on teaching adolescents the skills needed to handle relationships, resist peer pressures, and negotiate difficult situations. Although teens are using contraception much more frequently than in the past, and their preferred method—condoms—is widely available in stores, they do not typically

"Teenage pregnancy rates [in the U.S.] are still at least twice as high as in other industrialized countries."

use it consistently, especially when they are young. The result is that failure rates are high and unplanned pregnancies all too common. Even a 12 percent annual failure rate, typical for condom users, cumulates to an almost certain pregnancy in the dozen years between puberty and marriage or an adult job. Part of the problem is that the boys and young men involved are not held accountable for their actions. Although the welfare law puts considerable emphasis on establishing paternity and collecting child support from fathers, up until now, most have had a free ride. Unwed fathers need to be offered the same work opportunities and be subjected to the same requirements as the mothers of their children. And if Congress wants to do something about the so-called "marriage penalty," the place to start is with the Earned Income Tax Credit. As a result of the credit, a working single parent with two children can qualify for almost $4,000 a year. But if she marries another low-wage earner, she stands to lose most or all of these benefits. Congress should consider basing the credit on individual rather than family earnings. (A requirement that couples split their total earnings before the credit rate was applied would prevent benefits from going to higher-income families.) Under such a revised EITC, incentives to marry would be greatly enhanced.

In the meantime, efforts to equip adolescents with the knowledge and the means to avoid pregnancy in the first place have been highly charged politically and have created a backlash by conservatives, and even by some moderates, who want more emphasis placed on abstinence. Public opinion polls show that over 90 percent of the public believes that abstinence is the appropriate standard for school-age youth, even though a majority still wants contraceptives to be available as a backup. (Contrary to what some believe, there is no evidence that teaching young people how to protect themselves causes them to have more sex.) As part of the 1996 welfare reform bill, Congress provided $50 million a year for abstinence education programs. Such programs have never been adequately evaluated and many experts are skeptical that "just say no" campaigns by themselves will have much effect. But there is newfound appreciation for the need to encourage abstinence, especially among younger teens. In addition, if these or other funds were used for programs such as mentoring, community service, or after school activities, it could make a difference.

Those looking for guaranteed programmatic solutions to this problem are likely to be disappointed. The point is not that programs can't be effective, but that in isolation from a change in social norms, their impact may be small. Conversely, an intervention that begins by affecting behavior in quite modest ways may eventually produce changes in norms that snowball into bigger long-term effects. Behavior is contagious. Teens, in particular, are enormously influenced by what their friends, parents, and heros say and do, as documented in research commissioned by the National Campaign to Prevent Teen Pregnancy. This suggests that programs not be judged only on the basis of their immediate effects but also on their potential to reengage parents and reorient peer culture. It also suggests devoting some funds to media campaigns and to support for community or youth-led efforts that focus on values and not just services.

In conclusion, reducing teen pregnancy could substantially decrease child poverty, welfare dependency, and other social ills. Although little is known with certainty about how to advance this objective, states now have the opportunity to experiment with a variety of promising approaches that are critical to the longer-term success of current welfare reform efforts. Whatever approach states choose, they should remain cognizant of the importance of strengthening the social norm that teen out-of-wedlock childbearing is—to put it most simply—wrong.

Some Teens Benefit from Early Parenthood

by Emory Thomas Jr.

About the author: *Emory Thomas Jr. is a staff reporter for the* Wall Street Journal.

A high-school reunion turned economist Cecilia A. Conrad into a contrarian, at least on the issue of teenage pregnancy.

Teen Mothers Fare Well

She was an assistant professor at Barnard College in 1987 when she returned to the mostly black Dallas high school where she'd been valedictorian 15 years before. As part of a class that included a throng of girls who'd had babies as teenagers, Dr. Conrad wasn't surprised to find herself, at age 33, the only new mother at the reunion.

Yet Dr. Conrad was struck by how well many of her classmates had fared despite early and often out-of-wedlock motherhood. Almost none had sunk into prolonged poverty or welfare dependence, as conventional wisdom might dictate. One was a laboratory technician. Another was an inspector with the Food and Drug Administration. A third was a veteran Postal Service worker.

Back at Barnard, she puzzled over why she'd postponed motherhood while so many of her classmates hadn't—and how, rather than regretting having children at an early age, many seemed to count it a plus. Her questions led her away from an academic interest in business competitiveness and headlong into the emerging field of family economics. She eventually embraced a controversial but provocative theory: that many unmarried teens are having babies as a rational response to prevailing economic conditions—specifically the job market they face.

Dr. Conrad, one of a vanguard of academics who are examining the subtle economic forces shaping seemingly capricious life decisions, stresses that two-parent families tend to be best for raising children. But she poses an unorthodox premise: Teen pregnancy isn't always the disaster it's presumed to be; indeed, some disadvantaged teen mothers don't actually suffer at all economically.

Teen Mothers Earn More Money

Roughly one of every three births in America is to an unmarried mother, about 30% of them teenagers. Nearly 75% of all single teen mothers spend some time on welfare, and Congress is now considering denying or reducing such benefits.[1]

With the welfare debate as backdrop, Dr. Conrad and other family economists are looking at childbearing data in fresh ways. Sociologists tracking unwed mothers' outcomes have traditionally underplayed income factors when comparing teenagers with older mothers, and the teens overwhelmingly lag in schooling, employment and other criteria. But the vast majority of teen births come among the disadvantaged. By zeroing in on the culture of poverty—and the fate of mothers of different ages in it—other researchers are turning up quite a different picture.

University of Chicago Prof. V. Joseph Hotz, for example, found in a 1995 study that teenage mothers tend to earn more over their lifetimes, and have steadier employment histories, than similarly disadvantaged women who delay childbearing until they're 20 or older. Another researcher, Arline T. Geronimus, a professor at the University of Michigan, found in a 1994 study that, in impoverished conditions, the children of teen mothers tended to do as well or better than children of older mothers on cognitive, emotional and achievement tests.

> *"Teen pregnancy isn't always the disaster it's presumed to be; indeed, some disadvantaged teen mothers don't actually suffer at all economically."*

In poor African-American communities many teenage girls have relatively low expectations of marrying or finding more than marginal jobs, Dr. Conrad says. In such cases, traditional restraints on teenage passions are often absent. "Just saying you should wait, without making it more attractive to wait, isn't going to be very effective," she says.

Early Childbearing Is a Rational Choice

Dr. Conrad explains that a girl may observe that her unmarried sister, who has just given birth at age 27, has lost her job as a result and is having a tough time making ends meet. A 17-year-old friend with a newborn, meanwhile, is getting by, thanks to support from her parents, who are young and energetic enough to help with child care while she goes to school or finds work. (According to the Congressional Budget Office, about three-quarters of black adolescent mothers live with relatives in the two years after giving birth.)

The notion that unwed teenagers make a "rational choice" to have babies has drawn criticism from those who attribute the rise in unwed teen births to a

---

[1]The welfare bill passed by Congress in 1996 allows states to deny benefits to teenage mothers.

breakdown in moral responsibility, say, or lack of birth-control education. Another explanation: Teens drift into childbearing on the current of social customs that shift "like the width of ties or hemlines," says Frank F. Furstenberg Jr., professor of sociology at the University of Pennsylvania and a prominent teen-pregnancy researcher.

Teenagers themselves report an array of reasons for becoming pregnant: peer pressure, lack of birth control, fear of losing a boyfriend. Yet Dr. Conrad and others believe it boils down to how hard a teenager tries *not* to get pregnant. That underlying determination—or lack of it—is heavily influenced by her perception of economic possibilities, she says.

> *"In impoverished conditions, the children of teen mothers tended to do as well or better than children of older mothers on cognitive, emotional and achievement tests."*

Dr. Conrad, who recently moved from Barnard to another tenured position at Pomona College in Claremont, Calif., believes that her own decision to avoid early pregnancy was a function of the high expectations of her upper-middle-class family. Her surgeon father served on the Dallas board of education. Her parents compensated for deficiencies in the schools, at one point hiring a French tutor for her and a group of friends. After Franklin D. Roosevelt High School's class of 1972 voted her "most likely to succeed," she went on to graduate from Wellesley College and got her doctorate in economics at Stanford University.

Early Childbearing Makes Sense for Poor Women

For most students at Roosevelt, which is located in a lower-middle-class neighborhood, the path led in a different direction. Fellow 1972 graduate Jo Ann Williams recalls that she had neither the means nor family encouragement to attend college, and soon after high school she became pregnant.

Her parents helped care for her daughter while Jo Ann worked full-time in a clerical job, earning several promotions. If she had waited until her mid-20s to have a child, "I probably wouldn't have been promoted as fast or learned as much as I did," says Mrs. Williams, now married to the father of her child and working as an office manager at Dallas Water Utilities. "If I were to do it all over again," she adds, "I'd do it exactly the same way."

It's well-established, Dr. Conrad points out, that professional women are delaying childbirth in order to establish careers before temporarily dropping out of the work force. Her computer analysis of vital statistics and occupational data suggests that labor-market factors also influence birth-timing at the opposite end of the economic spectrum—and in opposite ways.

Today, the largest single occupation for black working women is clerical work (vs. domestic service, the top category in 1965). Because uninterrupted tenure tends to be the surest way to increase pay and benefits in the office-support labor market, Dr. Conrad says "it can make sense to have kids early" before taking such jobs.

Labor-market forces "certainly could be contributing" factors in explaining out-of-wedlock teen-pregnancy rates, says Gary S. Becker, the Nobel Prize-winning economist from the University of Chicago. But he speculates that the bleak job market may play a larger role with teen boys, in deterring them from marriage. Also, he cautions, such factors "are not 100% of the story."

Sitting in her office in Pomona College, Dr. Conrad observes that the parenting decisions made by some of her teen-mother classmates were "more rational" than her own. She and her husband, Llewellyn Miller, a risk-management consultant, decided to have a child soon after she joined the Barnard faculty. In retrospect, she says, "I should have waited until I had tenure."

The Decline of Teen Marriage Is a Serious Problem

by Patrick F. Fagan

About the author: *Patrick F. Fagan is a fellow in Family and Culture Studies at the Heritage Foundation, a conservative public policy research institute.*

The major change in teen pregnancy is not the numbers or rates of teen pregnancy but the massive abandonment of marriage among older teenagers, as well as among adults in their twenties. Ages 19 and 20 have traditionally been the highest fertility ages of women. That has not changed. What has wreaked the havoc is the abandonment of marriage, both before and after the birth of the child, and the abandonment of virginity and abstinence. The effects of the abandonment of marriage are major for the new offspring:

- Lowered health for newborns and increased risk of early infant death;
- Retarded cognitive, especially verbal, development;
- Lowered educational achievement;
- Lowered job attainment;
- Increased behavior problems;
- Lowered impulse control;
- Warped social development;
- Increased welfare dependency; some 92 percent of children on welfare today are from broken families.
- Increased crime in the local community;
- Increased risk of being physically or sexually abused.

Single Parenthood and Income

The presence or absence of marriage has massive effects on an individual's family income and on children's future capacity to earn a family wage, the external indicator of personal and family empowerment.

Testimony given by Patrick F. Fagan before the House Subcommittee on Empowerment, July 16, 1998, Washington, D.C.

The path to decent income is well known and traditional: complete school first, then get a job, then get married, then have children—in that order. A child's journey towards a steady income is enhanced by the intact marriage of his parents but can be stopped or lengthened by actions of his own, particularly not finishing school, not learning to work, getting pregnant before marriage, marrying too early, divorcing, cohabiting, having a child out of wedlock, and especially having a second child out of wedlock. Furthermore all of these actions weaken the prospects for the future of these children, and heighten the likelihood of the cycle being repeated within the next twenty years.

Out-of-Wedlock Births

Having a baby out of wedlock is the major way to derail progress towards a future stable family life with its attendant more comfortable domestic economy. It has great deleterious economic impact, for it takes a long time to overcome.

Teenage out-of-wedlock births have risen from 15% of all teen births in 1960 to 76% of all teenage births in 1994. Less than one-third of those who have a baby before age 18 complete high school, compared to the 50% completion rate for those of similar backgrounds who avoid pregnancy. However, . . . today the vast majority of out-of-wedlock births are to mature adults twenty and older, and births to teens below age eighteen are a small minority of all out-of-wedlock births. Furthermore almost half of all mothers who have one child out of wedlock have a subsequent child out of wedlock, further ensuring longer and deeper poverty.

> *"Having a baby out of wedlock is the major way to derail progress towards a future stable family life with its attendant more comfortable domestic economy."*

Unwed pregnancy exacts its price. Mothers who give birth outside of wedlock in their teens spend more of their lives as single parents than does any other group. As a result their children spend more of their time in poverty than do the children of any other group.

With both the single-parent family background and the poverty that accompanies it these children, in turn, will be twice as likely to drop out of high school, 2.5 times as likely to become out-of-wedlock teen mothers themselves, and be 1.4 times as likely to be out of school and unemployed. They will miss more schooldays, have lower education aspirations, get lower grades, and will divorce more as adults. They will be almost twice as likely to exhibit anti-social behavior as adults and be a quarter to 50 percent more likely to manifest behavioral problems such as anxiety, depression, hyperactivity, or dependence, and be two to three times more likely to need psychiatric care, or to commit suicide as teenagers. In short, the downward cycle will be repeated for many of their children.

Bleak Domestic Economics

The domestic economy young single mothers will be able to build for themselves and their children is bleak: over three-quarters of them will be on welfare within five years, and will comprise more than half of all mothers on welfare. In 1988 the average family income of children who lived with never married mothers was about 40% of that for children who live with either a divorced or a widowed mother.

From the research of Yuko Matsuhashi of the University of California at San Diego and his colleagues we know that few (14%) of the mothers live with both parents at the time of the first baby's conception, and almost none (2%) at the time of the second baby's conception. (This illustrates, by contrast, the powerfully protective influence of living with the intact family of origin.

> *"The vast majority of out-of-wedlock births are to mature adults twenty and older, and births to teens below age eighteen are a small minority of all out-of-wedlock births."*

Most of these teenage single mothers are themselves likely to have had parents who married early after pregnancy, or cohabited, or divorced, especially during the mid-teen years of the now young single mother.

Nearly 80% of the fathers do not marry these teenage mothers. Given the likelihood of similar family backgrounds and prospects for these men, the statement of demographer Larry Bumpass of the University of Wisconsin, in his presidential address to the Population Association of America makes sense: "If marriage assures neither a two-parent family for the child nor lifetime economic security for the woman, the importance of marrying to 'legitimate' a birth is much less compelling." Many more mothers of second out-of-wedlock babies plan to take care of their babies alone than do mothers of first babies, and much fewer of them live with their own parents. Fewer of the mothers can stay in school, lessening their chances of good income. In other words, single-parent domestic economies take deeper roots with the second baby.

Marriage, Virginity, and Child Poverty

Recently people have been rejoicing that teenage out-of-wedlock births and teenage abortions are down. Two very different changes are the likely causes: teenage virginity and Depo-Provera or Norplant. Teenage virginity is on the rise and mainline media report very high interest in the subject among teenagers. It is the new ingredient in the public discourse. Also, there are reports within the academic community that robust and very positive effects of virginity ceremonies are showing up in national survey data. On the other end of the spectrum of teenage sexual behavior the effects of the use of Depo-Provera and Norplant may also be leading to a reduction in the number of out-of-wedlock births among a very different set of teenagers, and is likely to be hailed by those who see marriage as irrelevant as their major hope for the future.

It is worth keeping in mind that despite its being overshadowed by the report's discussion of abstinence, the big news of the National Campaign to Prevent Teen Pregnancy's report, "No Easy Answers," was that despite thirty years of birth control education efforts, supported by the federal government and major foundations and academic institutions around the country, no birth control education strategy that clearly worked could be found.

These two approaches, abstinence and Depo-Provera lead to very different "lifestyles" and these lifestyles will likely have very different effects on young women and on their future families. Because it is investing in both approaches, it behooves Congress to know the differential effects of both strategies. The Institute For Youth Development has done excellent work in outlining the recent findings on the relative risk ratios for those who are sexually abstinent and those who are not.

There is virtual unanimity among researchers that family structure has a massive impact on income, and that children who grow up in intact married families have the best chance of empowerment, of economic independence in their adulthood.

Yet the restoration of marriage is rarely, and most frequently never, mentioned as a policy goal in the public discourse of many major institutions dedicated to relieving childhood poverty. Among all the major private foundations that have poured billions of dollars into research and programs to relieve childhood poverty, the restoration of marriage among our poor has received no attention. The same holds for the major private and public policy organizations dedicated to shaping public policy to help the poor. The same is true in the research institutions of higher learning, federal state and private. The same is true also of the federal government.

Given the overwhelming thrust of the research, given traditional wisdom, and given the desires of the poor themselves, this massive disconnect between the "advocates" and a large part of the solution is itself a major national problem. Any approach which ignores the major solution to a problem is not a strength but a weakness, not professional care but professional abuse. Past Congressional policy has ignored marriage and thus has not empowered our children but emasculated them.

Adult Premarital Sex Is a Serious Problem

by David Whitman, Paul Glastris, and Brendan I. Koerner

About the authors: *David Whitman, Paul Glastris, and Brendan I. Koerner write for* U.S. News & World Report.

Teen pregnancy, President Bill Clinton says, is the nation's "most serious social problem," and he has vowed to do something about it. The issue is a frequent "talking point" in his speeches, and, in an elegant White House ceremony in 1997 designed to underscore the administration's commitment, the first lady honored a dozen organizations for their work in tackling the problem.

For Clinton, as for politicians of every partisan stripe, lamenting the scourge of "babies having babies" is a no-lose proposition. Who could object? In preaching the virtues of abstinence during adolescence, however, the president and the first lady are not likely to mention one startling statistic: Many more 20-something adults than teenagers give birth to kids out of wedlock. In fact, most of the current social ills tied to sexual behavior—not only children born to unwed parents but sexually transmitted diseases, abortions, and the like—stem chiefly from adults who have sex before they marry, not from sexually active teens.

Adult Premarital Sex Is a Problem

In an "enlightened" 1990s America, where a person old enough to vote and serve in the armed forces is also deemed old enough to make mature sexual decisions, the elaboration of these statistics is sobering. In 1994, just 22 percent of children born out of wedlock had mothers age 18 or under; more than half had mothers ages 20 to 29. Over half the women who obtain abortions each year, most unmarried, are in their 20s, while just a fifth are under 20. And the same age disparity is evident among those who contract sexually transmitted diseases [STDs], including AIDS. Although a disproportionate number of teens contract STDs, only 1 in 3 reported cases of gonorrhea and syphilis in 1995 involved people under 20. Teen pregnancy is an urgent problem, hard on mothers and even harder on their kids. But teenagers account for a smaller proportion of unwed births today than 20 years ago. (As late as 1975, teen girls bore the majority of all out-of-wedlock children in the United States.)

Yet when it comes to the negative social consequences of premarital sex between adults, there is silence in the White House—and in every other political institution. Conservatives, quick to decry sex between unwed teens and outspoken on many other sexual issues, turn suddenly shy when asked about adult premarital liaisons. Among those who declined to be interviewed for this article were William Bennett, editor of the anthology *The Book of Virtues*; Gary Bauer, head of the Family Research Council and a former aide to former President Ronald Reagan; John Podhoretz, a onetime speechwriter for George Bush and deputy editor of the *Weekly Standard* ("he's really not comfortable talking about the subject," said Podhoretz's assistant); and Laura Ingraham, a CBS News analyst who was featured in a 1995 *New York Times Magazine* cover story on young conservatives.

> *"In 1994, just 22 percent of children born out of wedlock had mothers age 18 or under; more than half had mothers ages 20 to 29."*

Mum's the Word

The clergy, once loquacious on the topic of premarital "sin," are equally subdued. "Have you ever heard a sermon on 'living together'?" asks religious columnist Michael McManus in his 1995 book, *Marriage Savers*. Condemnation of adult premarital sex has virtually vanished from religious preaching, even in the homilies of Catholic priests. "In the pulpits there has been a backing away from moralizing about sex before marriage," says Bishop James McHugh, the bishop of Camden, New Jersey.

Why such reticence? The answer may seem obvious. Americans, at least tacitly, have all but given up on the notion that the appropriate premarital state is one of chastity. The Bible may have warned that like the denizens of Sodom and Gomorrah, those who give "themselves over to fornication" will suffer "the vengeance of eternal fire." Yet for most Americans, adult premarital sex has become the "sin" they not only wink at but quietly endorse. On television, adult virgins are as rare as caribou in Manhattan. Several studies have found that prime-time network shows implicitly condone premarital sex, and air as many as 8 depictions of it for every 1 of sex between married couples. And a *U.S. News & World Report* poll shows that while most Americans—74 percent—have serious qualms about teens having sex before marriage, more than half believe it is not at all wrong, or wrong only sometimes, for adults to have premarital sex.

Yet this surface consensus reflects a rather rapid—and surprisingly complex—transformation in American attitudes. The notion that sex ought to be reserved for marriage may now seem antiquated, but it wasn't very long ago that a large majority of Americans held just that belief. As late as 1968, for example, millions of Americans found it newsworthy that two unwed 20-year-old college students would publicly admit to living together. Newspapers and news-magazines replayed the tale of Linda LeClair, a sophomore at Barnard College, and Peter Behr, a Columbia University undergraduate, who conceded they had violated Barnard College's housing regulations by "shacking up" together in an off-campus apartment.

Love and Let Love

When Barnard students held protest rallies on LeClair's behalf, a beleaguered faculty-student committee relented and decided not to recommend her expulsion from the college. *Time* magazine warned darkly of LeClair's "moment of immoral victory." And William F. Buckley likened LeClair in his syndicated column to an "unemployed concubine." Even the tabloids purported to be shocked by the couple's open cohabitation, penning stories with headlines such as "Suffragette of Love and let-love" and "Nine-to-sex coed!"

Between that dimly remembered past and today's indulgence of sexual experimentation before marriage stand the arrival of the pill and the various skirmishes of the sexual revolution. As it turns out, if converting Americans to free love and loose sexual mores was the goal, the revolution was pretty much a dud. Despite the stereotype of the promiscuous American, most men and women are still sexually conservative in belief and practice. Just over 70 percent of Americans say they have had only one sexual partner in the past year, and more than 80 percent report they have never had an extramarital affair. For the past 25 years, there has been almost no change in how Americans view adultery, homosexuality, or teenage sex—a substantial majority think all three are always, or almost always, wrong.

In the aftermath of that turbulent era, however, there was one definite casualty: Americans' long-held conviction that virginity should be relinquished only in the marriage bed. To be sure, America has never been sexually pristine. Since the first settlers arrived, lots of unwed teens and young adults took a roll or two in the hay. And there was always a perceived double standard for men, who were expected to "sow their oats," and

> *"In May 1997, the U.S. government announced that the proportion of teens who reported having sexual intercourse went down."*

women, who were expected to save themselves for their husbands. Yet there are fundamental differences between the premarital sex of the 1960s and earlier eras, and that of the 1990s. In the mid-1960s, many more women were virgins at marriage than is now the case, and men and women who did engage in premarital sex often did so with their betrothed. Cohabitation was comparatively rare, and "shotgun weddings" for pregnant brides were common.

Almost certainly, television has had a central role in eroding the stigma of premarital sex. The sexual content of prime time has changed slowly, so viewers often fail to realize just how differently adult premarital sex is treated today from even a decade ago. Once, adolescents watched *Mork and Mindy*, the *Cosby Show*, *Little House on the Prairie*, and the like. Today, more than 6 million children under the age of 11 watch "family hour" shows that include *Beverly Hills 90210*, *Friends*, and *Roseanne*.

Sex, More Sex

TV's characterization of out-of-wedlock sex has also done a flip-flop. Sen. Daniel Patrick Moynihan might say that television's treatment of premarital sex is a classic example of "defining deviancy down"—what was once considered deviant or abnormal now is treated as the norm. In his book *Prime Time*, Robert Lichter and his colleagues at the Center for Media and Public Affairs found that prime-time television now by implication endorses unmarried adults' intentions to have sex in about 3 out of 4 cases and raises concerns only about 5 percent of the time. "On shows like *Three's Company* the characters hinted around a lot about premarital sex," says Lichter. "But the shows back then did not specifically seek to justify unmarried sex."

"The suggestion that abstinence is preferable to sex for unwed adults seems hopelessly retrograde."

Producers and screenwriters appear largely inured to this permissiveness, though viewers seem troubled. In a *U.S. News & World Report* poll in 1996, just 38 percent of the Hollywood elite were concerned about how TV depicted premarital sex, compared with 83 percent of the public. "Hollywood has glorified adult premarital sex," argues Sen. Joseph Lieberman. "And that is unhelpful if your goal is to reduce teen pregnancy and out-of-wedlock births."

In this climate, the suggestion that abstinence is preferable to sex for unwed adults seems hopelessly retrograde, about as timely as recommending that hansom cabs replace automobiles. It is virginity now that makes news. When a *TV Guide* columnist learned recently that college senior Donna Martin, the character played by Tori Spelling on *Beverly Hills 90210*, was scheduled to lose her virginity in the season's finale, the magazine issued a press release to detail this "scoop."

Majority Condones Premarital Sex

It is possible to argue that, on balance, the removal of premarital sex from the roster of moral or religious transgressions is a good thing. Certainly, most young singles believe they won't personally be hurt by premarital sex because they feel they use contraception responsibly. They minimize their own risk, on the assumption that unintended pregnancies, STDs, and abortions are problems that mostly afflict the careless.

In fact, the *U.S. News & World Report* poll shows that a majority of respondents under the age of 45 think that adult premarital sex generally benefits people quite apart from the issue of expanding their sexual pleasure. Unlike their elders, younger adults widely endorsed the sowing-one's-oats rationale for premarital sex, so long as the sowing is not done promiscuously. Less than half of those under 45 thought it was a good idea for adults to remain virgins until they marry. And a majority of respondents agreed that having had a few sexual partners makes it easier for a person to pick a compatible spouse.

America's acceptance of premarital sex also makes it easier to avoid rushing into marriage. By delaying family formation until after college, young couples escape being saddled with large loans and child-rearing duties while they are still trying to earn their degrees. And couples who wed for the first time after they turn 25 are less likely to be divorced a decade later than couples who wed while still in their teens. For all the nostalgia about the '50s, few Americans want to turn back the clock to that era, when about half the nation's women wed before their 20th birthday. Less than 8 percent of those surveyed by *U.S. News & World Report* thought it ideal for a woman to marry before she turns 20, and fewer than 5 percent thought it ideal for a man to marry before his 20s. The best age for a woman to marry, in most Americans' minds, is 24. For men, the ideal age is 25.

> *"The public willingness to tolerate and even condone premarital sex makes it much harder ... to curb other types of extramarital sex."*

Yet such "benefits" may be more wishful thinking than fact. Cohabitation may seem a good "trial run" for a solid marriage. But in practice, cohabiting couples who marry—many of whom already have children—are about 33 percent more likely to divorce than couples who don't live together before their nuptials. Virgin brides, on the other hand, are less likely to divorce than women who lost their virginity prior to marriage.

Sex Before Marriage Harms Traditional Values

Cohabitation is associated with other risks for young couples. Live-in boyfriends are far more likely to beat their partners than are spouses. And young adults who move in together, without being engaged to be married, are more likely to use cocaine and cigarettes after they start cohabiting than beforehand. All in all, muses Harvard sociologist Christopher Jencks, adult premarital sex "may ultimately prove to be a little like smoking dope in the 1960s. In retrospect, maybe it isn't so good for you after all."

In a broader sense, the public willingness to tolerate and even condone premarital sex makes it much harder for teachers, clerics, and law enforcement officials to curb other types of extramarital sex that are more controversial. Public acceptance of premarital sex has undermined the efforts of government officials to encourage abstinence among teens and to prosecute men who have out-of-wedlock sex with minors, and it has even colored the efforts of the clergy to keep gays and lesbians from being ordained. The Presbyterian Church (U.S.A.) recently enacted an amendment barring anyone currently engaged in extramarital sex—heterosexual or otherwise—from serving as an officer of the church. Put another way, sex before marriage has proved to be the runaway horse of traditional values. Once it took off, all the other old-time mores became more difficult to keep in their place.

An old joke among sex educators is that a conservative is a progressive with a teenage daughter. Few voters, with or without children, question that teens are generally less prepared to shoulder the consequences of sex than adults, or that there is an especially forceful case to be made for having teens—particularly younger adolescents—abstain from sex. Yet it is hard for parents to, say, convince a 17-year-old that she should abstain from sex now but that when she turns 18 or 21 it will be OK for her to start sleeping with her boyfriends. "I find it easy to distinguish between an adult with some emotional maturity and a 15-year-old having sex," says former Clinton White House aide William Galston, now a board member of the National Campaign to Prevent Teen Pregnancy. "Whether the 15-year-old will find it easy to make that distinction is another matter altogether. They may very well view it as hypocritical for a 45-year-old to say, 'Do as we say and not as we do.'"

Drawing a line between teen sex and adult sex is further complicated by the fact that many teenage women sleep with males age 20 and over, not with teen boys. Teen pregnancy is chiefly a result of these older men fathering out-of-wedlock babies with 18- and 19-year-old women, who are responsible for about 3 out of 5 teen births. Only a quarter of the men who impregnate women under the age of 18 are also under 18. As Mike Males puts it in *The Scapegoat Generation*: "If the president really wanted to prevent junior high sex, he would lecture grown-ups."

Fear of Hypocrisy

One renascent reform for curbing adult-teen sex is enforcement of statutory rape laws, which generally prohibit sex between girls who have not reached the age of consent (typically between ages 14 and 18) and older adult males. In the *U.S. News & World Report* poll, 64 percent of Americans said it was always wrong for a man over the age of 20 to have sex with a teenage girl. Both President Clinton and Bob Dole urged states last year to start reapplying the laws, and a handful have done so. But no state is seriously considering enforcing existing antifornication laws—which essentially prohibit consensual sex between unmarried adults.

Some of the reticence might be written off to the fear of seeming hypocritical, especially among younger conservative lawmakers: We had sex before marriage, so we can't suggest that others shouldn't—at least, not with a straight face. But the trepidation of those on the right has more complex roots, too. Conservatives with libertarian leanings believe that consensual sex between adults is a private matter, one the state shouldn't meddle in. About half those surveyed by *U.S. News & World Report* said unmarried couples who live together are "doing their own thing and not affecting anyone else." And at least some on the political right have come to accept the popular belief, echoed in the *U.S. News & World Report* poll, that premarital sex between consenting adults generally serves a positive purpose. As Richard Posner, a prominent conservative jurist and intellectual, puts it in his book *Sex and Reason:* "There is no good reason to deter premarital sex, a generally harmless source of pleasure and for some people an important stage of marital search."

Just what, if anything, can be done about the negative consequences of premarital sex is far from clear. Twenty years ago, former President Jimmy Carter told employees at the Department of Housing and Urban Development: "Those of you who are living in sin—I hope you'll get married." Carter's suggestion, Galston recalls, provoked "a massive horse laugh, particularly from the press corps." In 1997, state officials have begun to ponder how to reduce adult premarital sex in a formal way, owing largely to the new welfare law. During the Reagan and Bush years, Congress authorized several small "abstinence only" programs to teach high school students the benefits of abstinence, without offering information on birth control. The new welfare law sets aside $50 million for each of the next five years for states to fund abstinence-only programs. In toto, the U.S. government will spend about nine times as much on abstinence education in 1997–98 as in previous years. The vast bulk of the spending will surely be aimed at teens. But the programs funded in the welfare law need not be limited to them.

Willingness to Tackle the Problem

A second part of the new law deals more directly with the social ills that can attend premarital sex. It provides up to $100 million a year in bonuses for the five states that can show the largest reductions in out-of-wedlock births without corresponding increases in abortions. Since most out-of-wedlock births are to adults, state officials will, somehow, have to address premarital sex. Yet even conservatives aren't pretending they want the government to discourage most adult premarital sex. Their chief concern is out-of-wedlock births among welfare mothers, more than 90 percent of whom are currently 20 or older. "If the parents can support the child, fine; if they can't, then they ought to be discouraged from having it," says Posner.

The truth, for now, is that nobody has proven ideas about how to reduce adult premarital sex, nor has anyone shown much inclination to do so. The prospects for an en masse return to premarital chastity are almost nil, though some young singles may become more sexually conservative. In May 1997, the U.S. government announced that the proportion of teens who reported having sexual intercourse went down for the first time since similar surveys began in the 1970s.

The budding discomfort with casual sex is evident, too, in the enormous popularity of *The Rules*, the retro-guide that advises women how to coyly lure Mr. Right to the altar. Its authors don't counsel chastity. But they do advise "Rules girls" not to kiss a man on the first date and to put off sleeping with him for a few weeks or months. Jennifer Grossman, an MSNBC-TV contributor who is single, 30, and writes often on women's issues, argues that the appeal of *The Rules* among college-educated women reflects their search for a middle ground between casual sex and premarital chastity. "This all-you-can-eat sexual buffet is leaving a lot of men and women feeling very empty," she says. "I see a pattern among my girlfriends—when they sleep with men, they cry. Sleeping with a man you've known for a week is such an 'almost.' It's almost what you want—but a chasm away from what you really need."

In theory, more responsible use of contraception might provide another avenue for eliminating the worst complications of sex before marriage. In practice, though, the increased availability of contraception has not halted the rise in out-of-wedlock births or put an end to abortions and STDs. Adult premarital sex, the little-noticed heart of the sexual revolution, is here to stay. There may be little to do about this silent "epidemic"—except to acknowledge that sex before marriage may not always be the simple pleasure that many Americans assume it to be.

Chapter 2

What Factors Contribute to Teenage Pregnancy?

Chapter Preface

The factors contributing to rates of teenage pregnancy in the United States are many and complex. Some commentators argue that teen pregnancy is the result of a general breakdown in American society, while others contend that sexually explicit television shows and movies encourage teens to engage in sexual behavior that increases risk of teen pregnancy. Many argue that governmental programs aimed at reducing teenage pregnancy—such as condom distribution programs—actually encourage teens to have sex and increase the rates of teen pregnancy. Efforts to lower teen pregnancy rates are made even more difficult by the fact that these multiple factors tend to influence each other.

Poverty is a strong indicator for higher risk of teen pregnancy, for example, but lack of money alone does not encourage teen pregnancy; teenagers living in poverty are subject to many other influences related to being poor. Girls from impoverished areas often live in dysfunctional homes that provide inadequate love and support, for instance. Teens living under these conditions often try to establish meaningful intimate relationships outside the home, particularly with boyfriends. Frequently, these girls agree to early sex and use no contraceptives because they want to have a baby. As the *Atlanta Journal and Constitution* reports, the girls' "vision of the future is so impoverished that having a baby seems their only opportunity for status and emotional security." Billie Enz, a professor of social science at Arizona State University and an expert on teen pregnancy, claims that many poor girls grow up without a father and are especially vulnerable to coercive sex with older men. She writes, "They're looking for a father image that they can fall in love with."

Identifying the factors that contribute to teen pregnancy is made more difficult when the experts disagree. Not all researchers agree that poverty causes teen pregnancy, for example. On the contrary, many analysts contend that teen pregnancy causes poverty. Lloyd Eby and Charles A. Donovan argue that "teenage pregnancy has costs to the mothers, to the children, and to the larger society and nation" because teen mothers tend to fall into poverty. They claim that "73 percent of unmarried teenagers giving birth go on welfare within four years." Most members of families started by teen mothers, they contend, "are at very high risk of remaining poor and ill educated throughout their lives."

Efforts to decrease rates of teen pregnancy must consider not only the many influences on teens' lives but the interplay between those influences. In the following chapter, the authors examine several of the factors that contribute to teenage pregnancy, including poverty, sexual abuse, parental influence, drug and alcohol use, and exploitation by older men.

Sexual Abuse Is a Factor in Teenage Pregnancy

by Jacqueline L. Stock, Michelle A. Bell, Debra K. Boyer, and Frederick A. Connell

About the authors: *Jacqueline L. Stock is a research study manager at the Battelle Centers for Public Health Research and Evaluation in Seattle, Washington. Michelle A. Bell is associate professor at the University of Washington, Seattle. Debra K. Boyer is affiliate assistant professor of the Women's Studies Program at the University of Washington, Seattle. Frederick A. Connell is director and professor of maternal and child health services at the School of Public Health and Community Medicine at the University of Washington, Seattle.*

As sexual abuse of female children and adolescent pregnancy have gained increasingly widespread public recognition as problems in our society, the relationship between early abuse and teenage pregnancy also has become a focus of attention. However, differences in definitions of abuse, methods of inquiry and study populations have led to discrepant conclusions.

Some studies of adolescent mothers and pregnant adolescents have documented a high prevalence of sexual abuse, ranging from 43% to 62%. However, other studies of pregnant teenagers have reported a sexual abuse prevalence of 15–26%, rates no higher than those most commonly reported for the general population of women.

Sexual Abuse Can Lead to Pregnancy

Whereas data on a small group of college women suggested that those who had been sexually abused were at no higher risk for early pregnancy than their peers who had not been abused, findings from a population-based sample indicated that women who had been abused before age 18 were at increased risk of having an unintended pregnancy. Among a sample of women considered to be at risk for acquiring HIV infection, those who reported sexual abuse were three times as likely as those who had not experienced abuse to become pregnant before 18 years of age. In a study of sexually experienced adolescents, those who had ever been forced to have sexual inter-

Reproduced with the permission of The Alan Guttmacher Institute from: Jacqueline Stock et al., "Adolescent Pregnancy and Sexual Risk-Taking Among Sexually Abused Girls," *Family Planning Perspectives,* 1997, 29(5): 200–203, 227.

course were significantly more likely than others to have ever been pregnant.

While it is clear that forced sexual intercourse may directly result in pregnancy among pubescent adolescents, the path by which sexual abuse at young ages leads to teenage pregnancy is less direct and requires exploration. Consideration of the nature and context of a girl's early sexual experiences is necessary in understanding why some teenagers may be more likely than others to become pregnant. Premature, exploitive and coercive sexual experiences may form the social-emotional context for early pregnancy. Among the possible consequences of childhood sexual abuse are promiscuity and the self-perception of being promiscuous; being the victim of coercive sex later in life; and poor self-concept, low self-esteem and decreased locus of control.

> *"Premature, exploitive and coercive sexual experiences may form the social-emotional context for early pregnancy."*

Girls may be placed at increased risk for early pregnancy if they fear that they are unable to conceive. In a study of low-income, nulliparous adolescents [those who have never given birth], those with a history of sexual abuse were more likely than others to report that they were trying to conceive and feared that they were unable to do so. Although the nature of sexual abuse reported in various studies may differ in terms of type, duration, and relationship and age of the victim and perpetrator, any unwanted sexual experience and the perception of abuse contribute to increased sexual risk behavior and low self-esteem.

In this study, we hypothesized that a history of perceived sexual abuse is associated with adolescent pregnancy and predisposes girls to early pregnancy because of early initiation of sexual activity and other sexual risk factors. Our study goes beyond previous research in this area by comparing the pregnancy experiences of girls who have been sexually abused with those of girls with no history of abuse.

Methods Used in the Study

Study Population and Instrument   We analyzed data from the Washington State Survey of Adolescent Health Behaviors, which was administered to a sample of sixth, eighth, 10th and 12th graders in 70 school districts in December 1992. The survey used a multiple-choice format, giving students up to five possible responses to questions about their ethnicity, drug and alcohol use, health risk factors, sexual activity, and experiences of physical and sexual abuse. . . .

The final sample included 3,128 girls in grades eight, 10 and 12.

Data and Analyses   The questionnaire asked respondents whether they had ever experienced sexual abuse (defined as "when someone in your family or someone else touches you in a sexual way in a place you did not want to be touched, or does something to you sexually which they shouldn't have done"), whether they had ever been "physically abused or mistreated by an adult," and the number of times they had been pregnant. It also asked about alcohol consumption (quantity and frequency) and drug use (types of drugs and frequency of use).

Teachers administering the survey recorded students' grade level on the questionnaires. The following variables, which we hypothesized would be linked with a report of sexual abuse, were measured by students' responses to multiple-choice survey questions: ethnicity; parental supervision (how often the respondent's parents knew her whereabouts); number of school activities and sports teams the respondent participated in; how frequently she missed school; importance of grades; current grades; plans to attend college; thoughts of dropping out of school; body image; sexual experience; age at first intercourse; number of sexual partners; birth control method used during last intercourse; and suicide thoughts, plans and attempts. . . .

Results

According to respondents' reports, 5% were American Indian, 6% Asian or Pacific Islander, 3% black, 4% Hispanic and 82% white. Most (62%) were from urban schools. Respondents who did not have the opportunity to answer the questions related to sexual activity, suicide and abuse were significantly more likely than those in the final sample to be in eighth grade (59% vs. 38%), to be attending urban schools (84% vs. 62%) and to report that their parents always knew their whereabouts (38% vs. 34%). They were also slightly more likely to report no involvement in school activities (29%

"Sexual abuse was reported by 48% of students who had been pregnant at least once."

vs. 26%) and more likely to report no alcohol use (39% vs. 31%). There were no other significant differences between the two groups.

The prevalence of sexual abuse (with or without physical abuse) increased from 18% among eighth-grade respondents to 24% among 10th graders and 28% among 12th graders. Sexual abuse was reported by 48% of students who had been pregnant at least once and 21% of those who had never been pregnant. Some 60% of respondents who reported having been pregnant, but only 30% of those who had never been pregnant, had a history of any abuse (physical or sexual).

Sexual Abuse Associated with Other Problems

In analyses controlling for grade level, girls who had been sexually abused were significantly more likely to report a lack of parental supervision and a history of physical abuse. They reported significantly higher levels of school absenteeism, less involvement in extracurricular activities and lower grades than those with no history of sexual abuse; they also were more likely not to consider grades important, to have thought of dropping out, and to report they definitely or probably would not go to college. Other characteristics associated with a history of sexual abuse were alcohol and drug use, having thought about or attempted suicide, and poor body image.

In each grade, compared with respondents who had no history of abuse, those who had been either sexually or physically abused were approximately twice as likely to have been pregnant, and those who had experienced both sexual and physical abuse were about four times as likely to have had a pregnancy (Figure 1). Overall, when grade level was controlled for, respondents who had been sexually abused were 3.1 times as likely as others to have been pregnant. However, in a logistic regression model that adjusted for a variety of risk factors, many of which we found to be associated with a history of sexual abuse, the effect of sexual abuse itself on the risk of adolescent pregnancy was not statistically significant among respondents who had ever had intercourse.

Once we controlled for grade level, respondents reporting sexual abuse were 3.5 times as likely as those with no history of sexual abuse ever to have had intercourse. Moreover, in a logistic regression model controlling for grade level and other factors that increase the odds of ever having had intercourse (which themselves were significantly associated with sexual abuse), sexual abuse retained a significant effect.

The survey question "Have you ever had sexual intercourse?" did not rule out inclusion of experiences the respondents perceived as abusive. We have no way of knowing what proportion, if any, of respondents' reported sexual experiences were instances of abuse. Some 14% of eighth graders, 39% of 10th graders and 62% of 12th graders reported having had sexual intercourse. Since a broad defi-

Figure 1. Percentage of respondents who have ever been pregnant, by history of abuse, according to grade

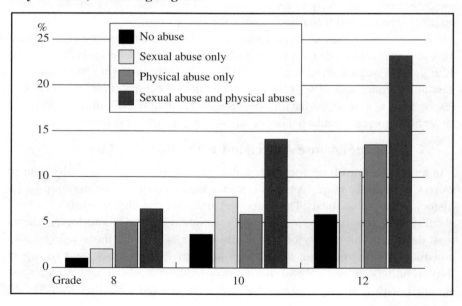

nition of abuse was used, it is unlikely that all of the reported abuse involved intercourse.

A history of sexual abuse was also a strong predictor of sexual behavior that increases the risk of teenage pregnancy. Respondents who had experienced abuse were twice as likely as others to have had first intercourse by age 15 (odds ratio, 2.1) and to have used no birth control during their most recent sexual encounter (2.0). They were slightly more likely to have had more than one sexual partner (1.4).

Comment on the Study

We found that sexual abuse was strongly associated with adolescent pregnancy, primarily through the strong association between sexual abuse and high-risk sexual behavior. The association between sexual abuse and adolescent pregnancy appears mediated in this way for two reasons. First, although a history of sexual abuse was strongly associated with reported sexual intercourse, it was not predictive of pregnancy among girls who had engaged in sexual intercourse. Second, when high-risk sexual behavior, which is strongly associated with sexual abuse, was added to a multivariate model, the effect of sexual abuse on pregnancy was no longer significant.

Clinicians and researchers who work with pregnant teenagers and adolescent parents have stressed that a better understanding of the social-emotional context of early sexual activity, especially premature or coercive sexual experiences, will contribute to understanding teenage pregnancy. Findings from this study suggest that premature and coercive sexual experiences contribute to adolescent pregnancy by increasing the likelihood that teenagers will have earlier sexual intercourse and a greater number of partners, and decreasing the likelihood that they will use birth control.

> *"Respondents who had been sexually abused were 3.1 times as likely as others to have been pregnant."*

Among a sample of female students in grades 6–12, one study found that 18% had experienced an "unwanted" sexual encounter. Another analysis, in which sexual abuse was defined as unwanted sexual touching by an adult or by an older or stronger person either outside or inside the family, found a sexual abuse prevalence of 17% among a sample of school-based adolescent females. Similarly, in a sample of school-based adolescent females, the prevalence of forced sexual intercourse was 13%.

The prevalence of sexual abuse in our sample (23%) is higher than the rates reported for adolescents in different geographic regions, but is consistent with findings from retrospective studies that use a definition of sexual abuse not limited to forced sexual intercourse. The prevalence of sexual and physical abuse (60%) among never-pregnant teenagers in this sample is similar to the prevalence documented for a sample of pregnant and parenting adolescents. The prevalence of sexual abuse among respondents who reported pregnancy (48%) is similar to that in other studies of pregnant adolescents.

Questions and Comparisons

The finding that respondents who reported sexual abuse were more likely than others to report a lack of parental supervision is supported by similar findings from an earlier epidemiological study. The overwhelming differences in negative social and health-related behaviors between the students who reported sexual abuse and those who did not expand upon findings from clinical or more limited samples and depict the sad accompaniments of sexual abuse.

Girls who either temporarily or permanently dropped out of school because of pregnancy were not included in the survey. Consequently, this sample represents only those who remained in or returned to school despite a pregnancy. It is possible that girls not in school at the time of the survey had different rates of sexual abuse and other risk factors from girls who remained in school.

Because this survey did not ask respondents the sequence in which pregnancy and abuse occurred, the abuse may have taken place after the pregnancy for some who reported both experiences. Biologically and developmentally, however, it seems more plausible that sexual victimization would have preceded pregnancy. Several epidemiologic studies have found that in the general population of women, 60–80% of incidents of abuse occur before 11 years of age, while 20–28% occur among adolescents. Studies of adolescent parents and pregnant teenagers have also reported young mean ages at first molestation (9.7 and 11.5 years, respectively).

We do not know whether this sample differs from other samples with regard to the age at onset of abuse or the proportion of girls abused during adolescence. In our sample, 18% of eighth graders and 28% of 12th graders reported a history of sexual abuse. This difference may reflect that as young girls age, they experience additional incidents of abuse, develop greater awareness of what constitutes abuse or become more willing to disclose prior abuse.

Sexual Abuse Is Often Underreported

A small number of respondents may have become pregnant as a result of abuse. For them, at least one incident of abuse may have been directly related to a reported pregnancy.

Further, because sexual abuse may be perpetrated by peers as well as older men, adolescent pregnancy may mask sexual abuse. Since the survey did not question respondents about the age of the perpetrator of sexual abuse, some may have reported on incidents involving peers. Consequently, findings must be interpreted according to a definition of sexual abuse that is not limited by the age of the perpetrator, but that encompasses any sexual experience perceived as forceful or coercive. However, in one analysis, the perpetrators of abuse were, on average, at least six years older than their victims, and many retrospective studies have indicated that perpetrators are at least five years older than their victims.

Some critics may question the authenticity of information regarding sexual abuse obtained via self-report. Cultural receptivity to reports of abuse has generally improved over time. Reasons for a girl not to report a history of sexual abuse far outweigh any speculations as to why one might falsely report sexual abuse on an anonymous survey. The tendency in reporting is to understate the prevalence of abuse. Further, the perception of abuse is equally important in predicting feelings of low self-esteem.

Sexual Abuse Has Costly Consequences

Maltreatment of any kind has been increasingly implicated as a strong factor in adolescent pregnancy. The fact that pregnancy rates in this sample were also high among girls who suffered physical but not sexual abuse illustrates the need for further study of how a history of physical abuse contributes to an increased risk of early pregnancy. It is notable that in analyses controlling for grade level and sexual abuse, physical abuse approached significance as a factor predicting pregnancy and was significant in predicting the likelihood of ever having had sexual intercourse.

> *"Coercive sexual experiences contribute to adolescent pregnancy by increasing the likelihood that teenagers will have earlier sexual intercourse."*

Also of importance is consideration of how nonparticipation in extracurricular activities could play a role in predicting pregnancy. Decreased participation may simply be a result of or concomitant with numerous predisposing risk factors. On the other hand, encouragement and support for girls to participate in activities may contribute to preventing early pregnancy.

Adolescent pregnancy is a multidimensional public health problem. Therefore, successful prevention strategies must address its many, complex aspects, including the important role of sexual abuse. Policy directives at the national level must set the stage for recognizing the costly consequences of sexual abuse. Thorough and routine inquiry regarding exposure to sexual abuse among school-age and adolescent girls may be helpful in targeting girls for prevention of teenage pregnancy, as well as for other needed counseling and support, particularly in the areas of sexual behavior and use of birth control.

Emphasis on primary prevention of undesirable experiences (for example, childhood and adolescent sexual abuse) would contribute to decreasing subsequent tragic and costly outcomes. The private nature of sexual abuse makes the task of primary prevention formidable, but crucial.

Poor Life Circumstances Are a Factor in Teenage Pregnancy

by Richard T. Cooper

About the author: *Richard T. Cooper is a staff writer for the* Los Angeles Times.

Scholar Joseph Hotz says teenagers do not have problems because they have babies; they have babies because they have problems. Instead of targeting teen pregnancy, society should address such causes as poverty and abuse of girls, he says.

Traditional Efforts to Fight Teen Pregnancy

With a fanfare of support from the White House and Capitol Hill, a coalition of liberals and conservatives called the National Campaign to Prevent Teen Pregnancy launched a crusade in May 1997. Its goals: to increase awareness of the devastating problems faced by adolescent mothers and to cut the teen pregnancy rate one-third by 2005.

Americans, the group declared, "see teen pregnancy as a powerful marker of a society gone astray—a clear and compelling example of how our families, communities and common culture are under siege." Experts warned of the link between teenage childbearing and multigenerational poverty, crime, joblessness and high welfare costs.

Hillary Rodham Clinton was host of a reception. MTV pledged to develop public-service announcements. Script writers and producers for ABC's daytime television shows offered to help. Black Entertainment Television lent a hand.

When the campaign was kicking off in Washington, Joseph Hotz's invitation must have been lost in the mail.

An economist and social policy specialist with a doctorate from the University of Wisconsin, 11 years on the faculty of the University of Chicago and a new faculty appointment at the University of California, Los Angeles, Hotz is the very model of a modern professional scholar. He was commissioned by a foundation fighting teen pregnancy to mount a major study of the issue.

But he came to conclusions that many in the fight against teen pregnancy and childbearing now wish would simply go away.

Hotz has found that being a teenager has almost nothing to do with the problems that afflict most such women and their children. Teenage childbearing is a symptom, he says, not a cause. Teenagers do not have problems because they have babies; they have babies because they have problems.

Even if they had put off having children for a few years, it would make little difference, Hotz contends. They would still be poor, still collect welfare, still have terrible jobs and difficult lives. Their problems are severe and began early in their lives. Focusing on their age diverts attention from the real causes of those problems, he says.

Underlying Causes

Hotz has amassed what some of his fellow scholars consider an impressive body of evidence. Professor Christopher Jencks of Harvard, a specialist in poverty, praises Hotz's research methods as "way better than anything anyone else has done before."

If Hotz should turn out to be right, the implications for national policy would be substantial: Instead of crusading against the symptoms, society should be working on the underlying causes—such things as poverty, dysfunctional families, physical and sexual abuse of young girls, poor school performance and behavioral problems.

For advocacy groups and others grappling with the problem, there are at least two inconvenient aspects to Hotz's message:

> *"Teenagers do not have problems because they have babies; they have babies because they have problems."*

First, it implies a need to help the teens develop more stable lives with the help of the government, which is politically unpopular these days. "It's easier to blame it all on the teenagers," said Linda Ohmans, whose experience directing a program for teenage mothers in Washington parallels Hotz's findings.

Second, Hotz's work implies that a great deal of well-intentioned effort by family-planning organizations, proponents of more sex education and other groups has been wide of the mark. Neither liberals nor conservatives view Hotz's findings with much relish; each side sees them as potential ammunition for the other.

"I understand that this is not what everyone wants to hear," Hotz said, "but sooner or later we've got to own up to the fact that some things are not likely to work."

Small wonder the professor was not sitting at the head table.

Hotz is not the first to question the idea that having a baby as a teenager causes the manifold problems that follow.

Arline Geronimus of the University of Michigan and Sanders Korenman of the National Bureau of Economic Research had already conducted studies casting doubt on teenage childbearing as the cause of later problems.

Hotz's breakthrough was to develop a method for comparing teenage mothers with a group of their peers—a formidable task because, even in the poor, minority neighborhoods in which most teen mothers live, they are significantly more disadvantaged than most other young women around them.

Surprising Findings

Hotz and his colleagues, using data from a study that has been following a large group of young women for many years, extracted a sample of women that had had babies as teenagers and another group that had become pregnant as teens but had had miscarriages and had children later.

When Hotz's team looked at how the lives of the two sets of women had turned out, some startling conclusions emerged:

- By their mid-30s, the teen mothers had worked harder and longer and earned more money than their counterparts who had their first babies later. Both groups had collected welfare, but the teen mothers had paid more taxes and on balance cost taxpayers less.
- The teen mothers got about as much education as their peers who deferred childbearing. Fewer graduated from high school, but more got equivalency diplomas.
- Problems of alcohol and drug abuse were no more common among the teen mothers than among the other group.

Even the children of teenage mothers may not do significantly worse than the offspring of similarly disadvantaged but somewhat older peers, Hotz said, though this point remains disputed.

What explains these findings?

First, the problems afflicting teen mothers are generally so serious that the passage of a few years does little to erase them.

Second, most teenage mothers belong to communities in which having children at a relatively early age is the norm.

Third, because poor, severely disadvantaged women must compete near the bottom of the labor market, where credentials are less important than steady performance, there may be benefits to getting childbearing out of the way early, when earnings potential is lowest.

What makes Hotz unwelcome is not so much his research as the politics of the issue.

Even moderates find little reason to trumpet Hotz's work. The National Campaign to Prevent Teen Pregnancy, for example, is laboring to find ways to sidestep the ideological conflicts and find practical strategies both sides can accept. Giving the spotlight to Hotz's work could stir controversy and make it more difficult to build such coalitions.

Parents' Attitudes Are a Factor in Teenage Pregnancy

by Brent C. Miller

About the author: *Brent C. Miller is a professor and the head of the department of family and human development at Utah State University.*

Over two decades of research confirms that families—and particularly parents—are an important influence on whether their teenagers become pregnant or cause a pregnancy. In a variety of ways, parental behavior and the nature of parent/child relationships influence teens' sexual activity and use of contraception. While parents cannot *determine* whether their children have sex, use contraception, or become pregnant, the quality of their relationships with their children can make a real difference.

Parent/Child Relationships

Parent/child connectedness. The overwhelming majority of studies indicate that parent/child closeness is associated with reduced teen pregnancy risk; teens who are close to their parents are more likely to remain sexually abstinent, postpone intercourse, have fewer sexual partners, and use contraception consistently.

Parental supervision. Most studies show that supervision and monitoring of teens' behavior by parents are associated with reduced pregnancy risk. Teens whose parents closely supervise them are more likely to be older when they first have sexual intercourse, to have fewer partners, and to use contraception. Some studies indicate, however, that "very strict" monitoring or psychological control by parents are associated with *greater* risk of teen pregnancy, suggesting that less intrusive supervision may be more effective.

Parent/child communication. Research on the effect of parent/child communication is surprisingly mixed—only about half the studies find that open, positive, and frequent communication about sex is associated with reduced teen pregnancy risk. A similar number of studies find no relation between parent/child communication and adolescent sexual or contraceptive behavior. And a few studies suggest that parent/child communication is associated with

Excerpted with permission from "Families Matter: A Research Synthesis of Family Influences on Adolescent Pregnancy," by Brent C. Miller, April 1998. Reprinted with permission from The National Campaign to Prevent Teen Pregnancy.

teens being *more likely* to have sexual intercourse. However, it is often not clear whether the communication predates the sexual activity or is a consequence of parents learning about teens' sexual activity. Studies vary greatly in how parent/child communication is measured and in whether other important variables—like parents' values—are taken into account. More and better research is needed in this area.

Parents' attitudes and values about teen sex. Although relatively few studies have examined the role of parents' values in influencing the sexual behavior of their adolescents, those that have suggest that teens with parents who hold strong opinions about the value of abstinence, or about the dangers of unprotected intercourse, are at less risk of teen pregnancy.

Family Influences

Interaction of connectedness, supervision, communication, and parental values. Of course, these parental influences work together to affect teens' pregnancy risk. For instance, if a teen feels strongly connected to his or her parents, he or she is probably more likely to go along with parental supervision, and the parents would be more likely to allow their child appropriate autonomy. Similarly, parent/child communication about sex is most strongly associated with reduced pregnancy risk when parents and children have close relationships and when parents disapprove of teen sex. Researchers believe that two factors help a child internalize parents' values: a parental message that is accurately received by the child and a willingness by the child to accept the message and allow it to guide his or her behavior.

Family structure and context. How a teen's family is structured and where the family lives are also important indicators of pregnancy risk. Children in single-parent families are more likely to initiate sexual activity at an early age. Teens with older siblings who are sexually active, have been pregnant, or have given birth are at higher risk of pregnancy themselves. Kids who grow up in abusive families are more likely to be sexually active and not to use contraception consistently. The social contexts of children's families can have an important effect on teen pregnancy risk, too. Teens living in neighborhoods beset by poverty, unemployment, and high crime rates are more likely to start having sex early, not to use contraception, and to become pregnant (or cause a pregnancy).

> *"Close, warm relationships between parents and teens appear to have the strongest association with reduced pregnancy risk."*

Family biological and hereditary influences. Family biological influences probably play a more important role in the risk of adolescent pregnancy than has generally been recognized. Several biological and hereditary variables—for instance, timing of pubertal development and hormone levels—are associated with adolescent sexual intercourse behaviors.

This research goes a long way toward confirming what many parents want to believe—that they can, and do, play an important role in reducing the risk of teen pregnancy for their kids. Close, warm relationships between parents and teens appear to have the strongest association with reduced pregnancy risk. And while parents' values and parent/child communication seem also to be important influences, better research on these factors is needed to clarify how they interact with parent/child connectedness and supervision.

New data from the National Longitudinal Study on Adolescent Health amplify several of the conclusions that emerge from the research literature review:

• Mothers and teens overwhelmingly report that their relationships are close.

• Seven in ten mothers say they have talked a moderate amount or a great deal about sex with their children.

• Almost 90 percent of mothers say they have discussed with their children at least somewhat the moral issues of not having intercourse.

• Eighty-three percent of mothers have discussed birth control at least somewhat with their children, with about one-third saying they've discussed it "a great deal."

Drug and Alcohol Use Is a Factor in Teenage Sex

by Susan Foster

About the author: *Susan Foster is vice president and director of policy research and analysis at the National Center on Addiction and Substance Abuse (CASA) at Columbia University, which studies how substance abuse affects society. Foster directed the CASA report on sex and substance abuse.*

A PBS [Public Broadcasting System] *Frontline* documentary chronicled an outbreak of syphilis among a large circle of teens in a suburban Atlanta community. What was even more alarming to health officials and the community was the revelation of a pattern of sex among upwards of 200 teens, focused around a group of girls, some as young as 13, with multiple partners, drinking and drug use, little if any protection, with no regard for the consequences.

Drug Use and Sex

The events in Georgia raise the question of whether this was an isolated incident or a harbinger of teen life around the country. What is certain is the disturbing connection between teen drinking and drug use and the increased likelihood of sexual activity.

A new report released last month by the National Center on Addiction and Substance Abuse at Columbia University (CASA) raises troubling concerns about substance use and teen sexual activity: Teens who drink or use drugs are much more likely to have sex, initiate it at younger ages and have multiple partners, placing them at higher risk for sexually transmitted diseases (STDs), AIDS and unplanned pregnancies.

The report, "Dangerous Liaisons: Substance Abuse and Sex," is the result of a two-year, unprecedented analysis of the connection between drinking, drug use and sexual activity. The report's sobering conclusion finds that in America, drinking and drug abuse are bundled with high-risk sex.

Before graduating high school, and even as early as middle school—among 10- to 13-years-olds—every teen will have to make a conscious choice whether

Reprinted from "Early Use of Booze, Drugs Leads to Sex and Problems," by Susan Foster, *The San Diego Union-Tribune,* January 23, 2000. Reprinted with permission from the author.

to drink or use illegal drugs and whether to have sex. Many teens will face all these decisions at once.

More Teens Are Having Sex

CASA's analysis shows that almost 80 percent of high school students have experimented with alcohol at least once. More than half had used at least one illicit drug. CASA's report noted the dramatic increase in just a generation of the proportion of 15-year-olds having sex: according to national surveys in 1970, less than 5 percent of 15-year-old girls and in 1972, 20 percent of 15-year-old boys, had engaged in sex. CASA's analysis reveals that in 1997, 38 percent of 15-year-old girls and 45 percent of 15-year-old boys have had sex.

Among the report's key findings:

• Teens 14 and younger who use alcohol are twice as likely to have sex than those who don't.

• Teens 14 and younger who use drugs are four times likelier to have sex than those who don't.

• Teens 15 and older who drink are seven times likelier to have sexual intercourse and twice as likely to have it with four or more partners than nondrinking teens.

• Teens 15 and older who use drugs are five times likelier to have sex and three times likelier to have it with four or more partners than those who don't.

> *"Teens are more vulnerable to the combined lure of sex and alcohol and drugs."*

Sixty-three percent of teens who use alcohol have had sex compared to 26 percent of those who never drank. Among teens who use drugs, 72 percent have had sex compared to 36 percent who have never used drugs.

Teens are more vulnerable to the combined lure of sex and alcohol and drugs. They are less able to cope with the potential consequences of drinking and using drugs which can undermine decisions about abstaining from sex, having unprotected sex and also trigger irresponsible and dangerous sexual behavior that can change the course of their lives.

Serious Consequences

The United States has the highest rate of STDs in the developed world. Teens are inconsistent condom users with or without alcohol and drugs which make the consequences of teen sexual activity linked to substance use clear: increased chances of infection by STDs such as syphilis, gonorrhea, chlamydia, as well as AIDS and unintended pregnancies.

While it is clear that teens who drink and use drugs are likelier to have sexual intercourse at earlier ages and with multiple partners, it is not clear which starts first—sexual intercourse or drinking or drug use. For parents, the point is that regardless of the sequence, either may be a red flag for the other. The report contains a loud and clear message for parents, clergy, school counselors and other caring adults: whichever teen activity—sex or substance use—first comes to their attention, these adults should be prepared to work with the teen on both matters.

Key to reducing a teen's risk of substance use is the power of parents. Parents have more influence over their children than they think. A CASA survey of 2,000 teens released in August 1999 showed that 42 percent of teens who don't use marijuana credit their parents over any other influence; teens who used marijuana say their friends are the primary influence in their decision to try the drug.

Teens Need Both Parents

The same survey stressed the need for both parents to be engaged and involved in their children's lives. Children living in two-parent families who have a fair or poor relationship with their father are at 68 percent higher risk of smoking, drinking and using drugs compared to the average teen. Teens consistently rate moms more favorably than dads: more teens report having a very good or excellent relationship with their moms, say it's easier to talk to mom about drugs, credit mom more with their decision not to use marijuana, and go to her more often when confronted with major decisions.

The safest teens are those living with two parents and who have a positive relationship with both.

CASA's earlier teen survey also found that teens who attend a school where drugs are kept, used or sold are at twice the risk of substance abuse as teens attending a drug-free school. Schools can also do their part by creating comprehensive and age-appropriate education programs that address the association between substance abuse and sex.

When it comes to sex and substance abuse, how parents exercise their power in talking to their children about drinking, using drugs and engaging in sexual activity will be critical in how their children respond to the lure of alcohol, drugs and sex—as will the messages they send by their own behavior. For parents who believe that sexual abstinence before marriage is a moral imperative, the report signals the particular importance of persuading teens not to drink alcohol or use illegal drugs. For those parents who consider teen sexual activity an inevitable or appropriate rite of passage, the CASA report points up the greater dangers for those teens who do drink and use drugs.

Exploitation by Older Men Is a Factor in Teenage Pregnancy

by Joseph P. Shapiro and Andrea R. Wright

About the authors: *Joseph P. Shapiro and Andrea R. Wright write for* U.S. News & World Report.

The problem with teen sex is not simply that teens are having sex. Adults, in disturbing numbers, are having sex with teens. It is not just Joey Buttafuoco and Amy Fisher[1], Woody Allen and Soon-Yi Previn[2] or the fact that O.J. Simpson was 30 when he began dating an 18-year-old waitress named Nicole Brown.[3] Federal and state surveys suggest that adult males are the fathers of some two-thirds of the babies born to teenage girls. According to the Alan Guttmacher Institute, 39 percent of 15-year-old mothers say the fathers of their babies are 20 years old or older. For 17-year-old teenage moms, 55 percent of the fathers are adults; for 19-year-olds, it is 78 percent.

Adult-Teen Sex

Little inspires more national hand wringing these days than the reality of teenage pregnancy. Americans blame impulsive kids and their raging hormones, ignoring the role of adult males. But in fact, teenage girls having sex with men is hardly a new phenomenon. In 1920, for example, 93 percent of babies born to teenagers were fathered by adults. What has changed is that more often than not, pregnant teens no longer marry the father. Today, 65 percent of teenage moms are unmarried, up from 48 percent in 1980. These teens and their children are at high risk of poverty, school failure and welfare dependency.

Welfare reform, sex education and teen pregnancy prevention programs are doomed to failure when they ignore the prevalence of adult-teen sex. The wel-

1. Buttafuoco was thirty-two years old when Fisher, his sixteen-year-old lover, shot his wife in the face in 1994.   2. Allen was thirty-five years older than college-aged Soon-Yi when he had sex with her.
3. Simpson was a pro football player who was accused of murdering Brown, his wife, in 1994.

fare reform bill passed by the House of Representatives would deny benefits to unmarried mothers under the age of 18, a provision that became one of the most contentious points of the 1995 debate in the Senate. [A modified version of the bill requiring unmarried mothers under the age of 18 to live in an adult-supervised home in order to be eligible for benefits was passed by the Senate in 1996.] But most studies suggest that curbing benefits alone will not stem the tide of teen pregnancies.

> *"Welfare reform, sex education and teen pregnancy prevention programs are doomed to failure when they ignore the prevalence of adult-teen sex."*

What drives teenage girls to become sexually involved with adult males is complex, and often does not follow the logic of Washington policy makers. In the minds of many teens, choosing an older boyfriend makes sense. Francisca Cativo was a 16-year-old high school junior when her daughter, Vanessa, was born in September 1994. Her boyfriend, Jose Confesor, is 24. To Cativo, who says she chose to get pregnant, Confesor's age was a plus; it meant he was more mature and more likely to support her child. "The boys around my age just want to be out in the streets playing around," she says. Still, on Confesor's salary as a part-time janitor, the couple is forced to live with his mother in a crowded apartment.

Older men seek out young girls for equally complex reasons—from believing there is less risk of disease to more chance of control. They often hold exaggerated power over their young companions. When teens get pregnant, for example, they are half as likely to have an abortion when their partners are 20 or older.

Coercive Sex

More disturbing, a sizable amount of teen sex is not consensual. Girls under the age of 18 are the victims of about half of the nation's rapes each year, according to Justice Department data. When researchers Debra Boyer and David Fine surveyed poor and pregnant teens at Washington State's public health clinics, they were startled to find that two-thirds of these girls reported prior sexual abuse, almost always by parents, guardians or relatives. Even more shocking: On average, the girls were less than 10 years old at the time of the first abuse while the offending male was 27.

Other adult-teen relationships simply blur the lines between unwanted and consensual sex. Eilene Stanley, who runs a Big Sisters teen-parent program in Tacoma, Washington, says girls—particularly those from broken families or who have been abused—are easy prey for men who show the smallest kindness, even something as simple as giving flowers.

"The justice system does not take care of these girls," complains Hazel Woods-Welborne, who runs a San Diego school program for teenage mothers. Police refused her request to invoke statutory-rape laws and prosecute a 51-

year-old man who had a child by a supposedly willing 13-year-old. Woods-Welborne is also disturbed by the recent increase in relationships between very young teens and older men: "I'm talking about 12-, 13-, 14-year-old girls. Most times, they cannot even spell intercourse."

The role played by older men raises doubts about pregnancy-prevention programs aimed at teens. "It's hard to teach teens about sex if one of the sexual partners is not sitting in the classroom," notes Kristin Moore of the research group Child Trends. She points to the adult-teen sex numbers as one reason why high school sex education classes have failed to curb teen pregnancy rates, which after several years of leveling off have been climbing since 1987, fueled primarily by increases among white teens. One answer, Moore says, is to extend sex education to where the boys are—to such places as vocational schools and the military.

Similarly, welfare reform can work only if it targets both teenage moms and their adult partners. Some legislative plans, including ones put forward by Senate Majority Leader Bob Dole and President Clinton, would give cash payments to pregnant girls only if they lived with a parent or another responsible adult [this legislation passed in 1996]. But to Tina in Tacoma, getting pregnant was a conscious decision that had nothing to do with the size of her welfare check. Tina left home at 15 when her parents objected to her 21-year-old boyfriend, Rocky. She says her parents would have insisted that she give up her son, Kevin, for adoption and end her relationship with Rocky. Three years later, Rocky and Tina plan to marry soon. Her child, she says, gives her the type of bond "I never had with my mom or with my dad."

Welfare reformers have recognized that adult fathers are more likely to hold jobs and be able to pay child support. Most welfare proposals would require hospitals to establish paternity at birth and then create a national database of fathers' names, so that men who refused to support a child would have their wages withheld or lose their driver's licenses. Yet there are limits to how much money can be collected: One Baltimore study found that 32 percent of the adult male partners of teenage girls were neither working nor in school at the time of a child's birth.

Still, teenage girls have become convenient scapegoats for what are really adult problems, argues Mike Males, a graduate student at the University of California at Irvine who has written extensively on adult-teen sex. Indeed, teenage pregnancy patterns are not that different from those adults: Rates of pregnancy among teens correlate more closely to class and ethnic background than they do to age demographics. Motherhood outside of marriage is on the rise for women of all ages. According to Child Trends, in 1991, for the first time, women over 20 accounted for more of the first births to unmarried women than did teenage girls. While single motherhood is becoming more acceptable for adult women, it remains a stigma for the unmarried teenage mother. As yet, there is little censure for the adult partners of these teenage girls.

Chapter 3

How Can Teenage Pregnancy Be Prevented?

Chapter Preface

Many social scientists argue that traditional approaches to reducing teen pregnancy rates—such as comprehensive sex education or abstinence-only sex education—have failed. They also maintain that new law-and-order approaches, such as enforcing statutory rape and fornication laws, are ineffective as well. Most teens who become pregnant, they contend, feel discouraged and lack healthy relationships with their families and strong connections with their communities. These critics assert that in order to lower the rates of teenage pregnancy, teens must develop a sense of connection and hope.

One program that works to bolster teens' self-esteem and help them develop caring relationships with others is Teen Outreach. Some of the activities in which the teens participate—such as field trips to homes for crack babies, for example—are designed to give them a more realistic understanding of child raising. Most of the activities—such as picking up trash—are not related to pregnancy in any way, however. Proponents of the program argue that any kind of voluntary service helps build a teen's self-confidence and connection with others. Joseph Allen, a professor of psychology at the University of Virginia, reports that teens in the program "had 40 percent fewer pregnancies than a control group of adolescents" who did not participate.

Many sex education experts believe, however, that teens need more than just community involvement programs in order to prevent pregnancy. Debra Haffner, president of the Sexuality Information and Education Council of the United States (SIECUS)—which provides sex education materials for public schools—argues that "there is no one magic bullet to prevent teen pregnancy." Comprehensive sex education programs, for example, present teens with broad information on how to use contraceptives to prevent pregnancy, how to say "no" to sex, and how to engage in sexual activity without intercourse. Proponents of comprehensive sex education programs contend that teens will engage in sexual activity; therefore, the most effective way to prevent pregnancy is to teach them how to have sex responsibly.

Conservatives who support abstinence-only sex education programs also maintain that community service programs are not sufficient in preventing teenage pregnancy. They argue that teenagers need to be taught that the only way to prevent pregnancy is to abstain from all sexual activity. Katherine G. Bond, a counselor for a crisis pregnancy center, claims that a 1996 study "indicated a 54 percent decrease in sexual activity after teens were exposed to [abstinence-only] curriculum."

There is much contention about which programs work best to reduce the rates of teen pregnancy. The authors in the following chapter debate some of these approaches.

Abstinence-Only Sex Education Can Prevent Teenage Pregnancy

by Vanessa Warner

About the author: *Vanessa Warner is a special projects' writer for Concerned Women for America, a public policy woman's organization that seeks to restore the family to its traditional roots.*

> *"In real life, the unheralded, seldom discussed world of married sex is actually one that satisfies people the most."*

Our nation's young people are bombarded with messages to engage in sex outside of marriage by educators, health workers, government officials, entertainment and news media outlets. However, most Americans *support* abstinence for teens—even if they take precautions against disease and pregnancy, according to a survey by the National Campaign to Prevent Teen Pregnancy. It has become increasingly clear that unbridled sexual activity is ravaging our youth and our land: sexually transmitted diseases (STDs), AIDS, abortion, out-of-wedlock pregnancy, fatherlessness, crime, welfare, violence and poverty. The solution for 21st century America? Abstinence.

The Myth of "Safe Sex"

Former U.S. Surgeon General Jocelyn Elders made her position on adolescent and teen sexuality quite clear in the statement, "We taught them what to do in the front seat, now let's teach them what to do in the back seat." That often included the distribution of mint flavored condoms, oral contraceptives and intrauterine devices (IUDs)—and campaigns to teach minors about so-called "safe sex" practices. This ideology also infiltrated our local school systems and percolated into our national consciousness.

Planned Parenthood and the Sexuality Information & Education Council of the United States (S.I.E.C.U.S.), in addition to other groups, routinely spread misinformation about sex and encourage youthful sexual experimentation. Oral

Reprinted from "Abstinence: Why Sex Is Worth the Wait," by Vanessa Warner, July 1998. Reprinted with permission from Concerned Women for America. Article available at www.cwfa.org.

sex, "outercourse" (sex without penetration), mutual masturbation, French kissing, fondling, and sex with a condom are all suggested as a means to *safely* explore one's sexuality. But are they really medically safe?

According to the latest report issued by the Institute of Medicine, a branch of the National Academy of Sciences, "STDs represent a growing threat to the nation's health, and national action is urgently needed." "The Hidden Epidemic" documents 12 million new cases of STDs annually, three million of them among teenagers. The director of the Centers for Disease Control and Prevention (CDC) has described the report as "a call to arms."

The CDC has announced that AIDS is the second leading killer of adults ages 25 to 44. Last year, it was the number one cause of death. Health officials at the CDC attribute the decrease to *fewer teens having sex.*

AIDS Deaths Will Rise Again

Although the new wave of protease inhibitors, called "cocktail" drugs, has prolonged the life of many AIDS patients, "there is an increasing percentage of people in whom, after a period of time, the virus breaks through," said Dr. Anthony Fauci, director of the Bethesda-based National Institute of Allergy and Infectious Diseases. "People are quite well for six months, eight months, or a year, and after a while, in a significant proportion, the virus starts to come back," he added. The fact that strains of HIV develop resistance to medical treatment virtually guarantees that the morbidity rate from AIDS will climb again in the future.

Added to these alarming statistics is the first documented case of HIV transmission from deep kissing. In February 1996, the CDC learned of a woman who contracted the virus from kissing an infected man. It is believed that the AIDS virus was transmitted through the man's bloody gums, not saliva.

The CDC's official policy is to encourage people who have had "unprotected sex with a member of a risk group" to be tested. However, Dr. Scott D. Holmberg of the CDC added that those who have engaged in French kissing with a person whose HIV status is unknown are urged to be tested for the virus as well. Although the CDC continues to alert people to the danger of deep kissing an infected man or woman, it has not recommended against French kissing in general.

> *"The spread of AIDS is essentially driven by behavior, and can best be combated through behavior modification."*

In attributing the decrease in AIDS to a rise in teen abstinence, the CDC publicly acknowledged what we have known all along—the spread of AIDS is essentially driven by behavior, and can best be combated through behavior modification. However, everyone from health officials, to school administrators, to policy "experts," continue to treat the disease, which is a symptom—not the root problem of promiscuity.

71

Condoms and STDs

In 1997, a gang of middle class teenage boys, called the "Spur Posse," competed with each other in a sexual game for "scores" which reflected the number of young women with whom they had sex. Many of these boys' scores reached into the 50s and 60s. When the "game" was discovered and came under attack, one young man involved remarked, "They teach us condoms this and condoms that, but they don't teach us any rules."

Our young people are paying an enormous price for our casual attitude toward sex and morals—some with their very lives. As Americans, we have abdicated our responsibility to train future generations to respect themselves, to honor their commitments, and to build strong families. The resulting fissure of disease and death will eventually swallow up our entire nation if we continue to bury our heads in the sand and throw condoms at the problem.

Studies have shown that condoms are not always effective at preventing pregnancy and sexually transmitted diseases including HIV. Moreover, herpes, syphilis and the "silent" STDs, such as chlamydia and the human papilloma virus (HPV), can be spread to men and women through contact with the *skin* of an infected individual—something condoms can't guard against.

These diseases often remain undetected, seriously impairing the health and fertility of males and females. Gonorrhea in men can lead to the blockage of the urethra (tube which carries urine and semen), often requiring surgery to rebuild. An infection from chlamydia and gonorrhea can result in pelvic inflammatory disease in women, leading to infertility, painful

> *"From 1970 to 1990, births to unmarried teens increased 90 percent, and the total number of such births has more than tripled since 1950."*

bowel movements, ectopic pregnancy and sometimes early death due to tubal ruptures during pregnancy. HPV causes genital warts in men and women and is the leading cause of cervical, vulva, and penile cancer. In fact, one of the primary reasons gynecologists recommend annual pap smears for women is to identify and treat pre-cancerous or cancerous cells caused by HPV. Unfortunately, the public continues to be misled about the effectiveness of condoms and the safety of what has been dubbed "serial monogamy."

Promiscuous Sexual Activity

"Social legitimization of promiscuous sexual activity has probably been one of the major stimuli for the proliferation of sexually transmitted diseases." It has been documented that engaging in coitus [intercourse] from an early age increases one's risk of contracting an STD by the age of 30 due to: 1) increased number of sexual partners, and thus, exposure to their STDs, and 2) greater susceptibility of young adults. As a result of such indiscriminate sexual activity, "[a]n estimated two-thirds of all cases of sexually transmitted disease occur in persons younger than age 25, and every year more than three million teenagers are affected."

It's clear there is a mounting public health crisis. In an age of condoms and sophisticated forms of penicillin, instances of gonorrhea, syphilis, and chlamydia are increasing. Not only are more and more individuals becoming infected, but drug-resistant strains of these viruses are cropping up. The situation is worsened by the transmission of other diseases such as pubic lice and hepatitis B.

> *"Teens who have children out-of-wedlock are more likely to end up at the bottom of the socio-economic ladder."*

Can we continue to believe that sexual activity outside of marriage is the best choice for an individual or society? The human body is not intended to function in this manner without facing serious, debilitating, and sometimes, deadly consequences.

The Cost of Illegitimacy

The sexual revolution of the 1960s ushered in a new era of "free love." Suddenly it became acceptable—even fashionable—for teens and adults to engage in pre-marital sex. Marriage was considered a dirty word, and children a liability. Sex became a cheap commodity without love or responsibility.

Not surprisingly, "from 1970 to 1990, births to unmarried teens increased 90 percent, and the total number of such births has more than tripled since 1950." It is estimated that by the year 2000, "40 percent of all American births and 80 percent of minority births will occur out of wedlock." These are alarming statistics. Because babies born to teens usually suffer from low birth weight due to poor pre-natal care, they require extensive hospitalization and costly medical attention—all financed by tax dollars.

This trend has led to an unprecedented breakdown of the family, the building block of a healthy society. Women and children are its primary victims. It is reported that half the households headed by single parents are below the poverty line. Not only are fathers absent in 90 percent of these homes, but they have abandoned all financial responsibility for the care of the woman and the child to the state. Consequently, largely uneducated, unskilled women are left to parent children without the traditional support of a husband and are dependent upon the welfare system for economic sustenance.

Social Costs of Teen Pregnancy

"About 50 percent of all unwed teenage mothers go on welfare within one year of the birth of their first child. More than 75 percent go on within five years." Taxpayers spend billions of dollars each year to support families like these with welfare, Medicaid and Food Stamps. And studies show that children born out-of-wedlock are more likely to repeat the cycle.

However, these are not the only societal costs. According to Alvin Poussaint, "when teenagers have babies both mothers and children tend to have problems—health, social, psychological and economic. Teens who have children out-of-wedlock are more likely to end up at the bottom of the socio-economic ladder . . . These numbers have enormous economic implications for the country—and for the rearing of children in America."

Since research indicates that most teenage mothers are impregnated by older males, it is necessary that we combat teen pregnancy by vigorously enforcing existing statutory rape laws. Statutory rape laws can act as an effective deterrent to males who would otherwise prey upon young girls. "For too long, society has turned a blind eye to the problem of adult men preying on young girls and engaging in unlawful sexual activity with them. Let there be no mistake: Statutory rape is against the law," said Delaware Governor Thomas R. Carper. Even former U.S. Senate Majority Leader Bob Dole (R-KS) and President Bill Clinton have called for the states to apply statutory rape laws. It is time that we aggressively pursue this course as a nation.

Failure of Trial "Marriage"

For years, couples have been encouraged to live together prior to marriage in order to determine their level of compatibility and to decrease the likelihood of divorce. However, studies have shown that couples who cohabit have a *33 percent higher incidence of divorce.* Thus, "shacking up" neither heightens commitment nor reduces marital failure.

People are not like cars that can be test driven. And trial "marriage" by definition signifies a lack of commitment to resolving conflicts and loving another person in sickness or health and for richer or poorer. The most solid marriages and faithful partners are found among those who save both sex and living together until after marriage.

Commitment is defined as "a pledge to do something." Marriage is, of course, founded upon that commitment. Thus, the term "trial marriage" is an oxymoron and statistics bear this out.

According to a Justice Department study of domestic violence against women between 1979 and 1987, husbands account for only a small percentage of abusers. On the contrary, boyfriends, ex-boyfriends and ex-spouses account for almost 65 percent of all domestic violence against women as compared with 9 percent husbands. It has also been documented that unmarried pregnant women are three to four times more likely to be assaulted by their boyfriends than by their husbands. It is obvious that a man who does not love a woman enough to marry her does not truly value or respect her.

> *"A close, loving parent-child relationship . . . is the greatest determinant of future behavior."*

Chapter 3

Quasi-Families

The same is true about destructive patterns of substance abuse. Studies have shown that unmarried men and women are less likely to curb their use of cocaine and cigarettes. However, there is greater incentive in marriage, with reports of people foregoing harmful addictions in order to please a mate and preserve a marriage. That is because without commitment, there is no obligation.

As Harvard sociologist Christopher Jencks said with regard to adult premarital sex, "[It] may ultimately prove to be a little like smoking dope in the 1960s. In retrospect, maybe it isn't so good for you after all." Trial "marriage" certainly has not been the blessing that everybody thought it would be, neither for the men and women involved in these casual relationships nor for the children born into these quasi-families.

Keys to Raising Kids Who Wait

It is essential that we understand that kids today want the insight and direction that only parents can impart as they mature and make the transition into the adult world. If, however, that is lacking, they will search for significance, identity, and approval by engaging in high risk behavior, which frequently includes sex.

> *"[Abstinence] needs to be taught in the context of other values such as self-control, responsibility, self-respect and building intimate relationships without . . . sex."*

Studies of inner-city black teenagers and mothers indicate a strong correlation between the parent-child relationship and premarital sexual activity. It was discovered that "when relationship satisfaction was high, when the mother was seen as being opposed to premarital sex and when discussions of birth control were minimal, it was 12.5 times more likely that the adolescent would not engage in sexual intercourse than when relationship satisfaction was low, the mother was seen as more equivocal in her opposition to premarital sex, and the mother had talked to a greater extent about birth control."

These findings have been greatly amplified by the federal government's 1997 National Longitudinal Study of Adolescent Health, the largest study ever undertaken of American youth. Researchers concluded that developing and maintaining a close, loving parent-child relationship, even though teenagers may appear to need or want less supervision and attention at this age, is the greatest determinant of future behavior. Parents have far more influence over their children's attitudes and beliefs than they are often credited with—or even realize. The key is to focus on cultivating a relationship and setting clear guidelines on premarital sex. Abstinence, it has been proven, is best communicated by limiting discussions about birth control and encouraging teens to wait, regardless of whether the child comes from a single or two-parent household.

Aside from setting high standards in the home and building positive relationships with teenagers, it is important that parents help their teens develop a healthy sense of self-esteem. Teens' motives for early sexual activity are not always purely sexual. Many are searching for a sense of love and security that they are lacking at home. Early sexual experience may destroy their level of self-esteem, but "delaying first coitus or choosing abstinence as a birth control method can be both empowering and ego-enhancing."

Parents Are Important

Parents can point teens to positive outlets for building confidence and teaching them how to make wise decisions. It has been reported that teenage girls are less likely to become pregnant when involved in volunteer work. "[T]eenagers engaged in community service gain the self-respect that helps them avoid bad choices." This is not surprising considering that for most girls their first sexual encounter was consensual, "but not wanted." It is thus the responsibility of parents and educators to give them healthy alternatives to sex, and to equip them to say "no."

Chastity rings and key chains are means to help teens commit to abstinence. Parents might plan a special outing for their teens to share their expectations about abstinence and to present them with the gift of a ring or key chain as a sign of the commitment they are making to save sex for marriage. It is important that parents use this time to listen to their children and discuss the benefits of waiting.

Study after study has also shown that religion acts as a deterrent to early sexual activity. In one survey of teenagers, it was discovered that "for both males and females, religious mores against premarital sex carried *more* weight than those posed by family." Again, it was found that "[h]aving a religious affiliation and attending religious services are inversely associated with earlier first sexual intercourse. . . ." Even a government study released in 1997 attributed an increase in teen abstinence to the influence of religious

> *"Saving sex for marriage actually enhances one's love life."*

beliefs. Consequently, parents, teachers and lawmakers should view religion as a positive aid in teaching children the virtues of abstinence and self-control—especially, since it appears to have *more* of an influence upon teens' behavior than any other single factor.

Saving Sex

Parents are just one part of the equation in promoting abstinence. It is also vitally important that teachers, health workers, public figures and lawmakers join together to equip teens with the tools necessary to say "yes" to relationships and "no" to sex.

Kate Schindle, Miss America 1997, has crossed the nation promoting "safe

sex" to our teenagers. But, her message is sending the wrong signal to impressionable children. What our nation's youth are learning is:
- You can't really be expected to exercise self-control.
- The risks of pregnancy and STDs, including AIDS, are negligible.
- Sex is meaningless anyway.
- Everybody's doing it, why aren't you?

This is borne out by research which shows that knowledge about sex, HIV and contraceptives alone does not change behavior. In fact, it actually acts as an impetus to early sexual activity.

We need a sound abstinence education policy. According to Helene Gayle, director of the U.S. Centers for Disease Control and Prevention, *abstinence* is *the best precaution* against HIV and other STDs. We already counsel people not to drink and drive and to quit smoking. Why are we still clinging to outmoded sex education strategies that have failed our young people and are decimating our nation?

Abstinence Education

In a day and age where the "lifetime" average number of sexual partners for college students is already four or five, our young people need to be taught that the sexual choices they make will have real and lasting consequences. Approximately one in four young people will become infected by an STD by age 21, and a staggering one-fifth of all AIDS cases in the U.S. are caused by HIV infections contracted by people during the teenage years.

Abstinence should not be presented as what happens between dates or relationships, but as a lifestyle. In order to be effective, this needs to be taught in the context of other values such as self-control, responsibility, self-respect and building intimate relationships without the physical and emotional entanglements of sex. "[G]iving young people skills to be able to resist social and peer pressures that lead them into early sexual involvement before they either want to become sexually involved or are ready to handle all the responsibility that should go along with a sexual relationship can be the most important educational component to add to basic fact giving."

Our society and culture is forcing teenagers to assume sexual roles for which they are not prepared. Despite the number of teens engaging in early coitus, an overwhelming number of males and females said they "respected," "approved," and considered as "smart" girls and boys who "decided not to have sexual intercourse until they were older or married." This is a clear indication that we are failing our young people by failing to offer them the clear moral guidance for which they are desperately searching. We have started them on the path of promiscuous sex instead of encouraging them to pursue lifelong love.

There are several problems with this. Marriage is actually rated more highly by virgins or people who have had only one sex partner than non-virgins, especially those who have had multiple sex partners. Thus, traditional families, a nexus of stability and personal development, are the ultimate casualties of this unrestrained attitude toward sex. Men and women also pay the price in unfulfilled dreams, uncommitted lovers, children fathered by many different men, and a general societal disconnect—the cost of discovering the sad truth behind the myth of the "happy" swinging single.

We need to restore the truth about marriage. "Teenagers [should] be taught that marriage is enjoyable rather than difficult and that it does not involve either undue responsibility or unwarranted sacrifice of personal freedom and happiness." It is also important that they learn that married sex satisfies the most—physically, mentally and emotionally. According to the authors of *Sex in America*:

> The relationship between being married and having orgasms during sex with a partner was very strong. Married women had much higher rates of usually or always having orgasm. . . . Those having the most partnered-sex and enjoying it the most are the married people. . . . The least satisfied [with sex] [a]re those who [a]re not married, not living with anyone, and who ha[ve] at least two sex partners.

Second Virginity

Marital sex studies by both *Redbook*, the popular women's magazine, and Family Life Seminars found that not only did married couples enjoy sex the most, but that religious people in particular had the highest sexual satisfaction of any other group in terms of the pleasure derived from the intimacy, orgasms and frequency of sex. This is further indication that saving sex for marriage actually enhances one's love life. There is simply no match for the level of love, commitment and tenderness expressed in the marital sexual relationship.

For those who have already engaged in sex, it must be stressed that it is never too late to postpone future sexual activity. Pop star Toni Braxton has announced that she is practicing second virginity—abstinence until marriage. It is the most effective means of protecting oneself from disease, infertility, and early death from AIDS, cervical cancer, ectopic pregnancy, and abortion. In addition, it decreases the emotional baggage in the future marital relationship.

The maxim, "You have sex with every other person your partner has ever had sex with," could also be applied to relationships in general. Every sexual encounter represents a piece of one's heart that has been given—often thrown—away, and a part of another person that will remain to burden future relationships. Committing oneself to a second virginity is not easy in this sex-saturated culture. But it will free our nation's singles to pursue their own goals and dreams and better prepare them for the ultimate love experience—marriage.

Title XX Funding

In 1996, 250 million dollars over a 5-year period has been earmarked by the federal government to fund abstinence-only programs in the states. Two of the grant provisions state that sexual activity in "the context of marriage" is to be the standard and that children are to be warned about the harmful "psychological and physical effects" of sex outside of marriage. This is an important victory in the battle for truth in our nation's sex education programs.

Researchers have concluded that: 1) sex education is "[not] effective in increasing teenage contraceptive use and reducing adolescent pregnancy" and 2) facts about sex without lessons in self-control actually increase a child's curiosity and tendency to engage in sex.

Abstinence training works—even in the inner city, according to a 1996 study published by Family Planning Perspectives. This merely reiterates what advocates of abstinence education programs knew all along: Abstinence is the *only* way to go.

It's time to stand for our nation's children. Together, we can educate state legislators and local school boards about this new government program and encourage them to adopt abstinence-only curricula. Our children deserve a chance for a future that includes more than sex without love or responsibility, out-of-wedlock pregnancies, STDs and AIDS.

Abstinence for America

There is a reason society has traditionally channeled sexual activity into marriage. Unbridled sexual activity wreaks havoc. This is not simply an issue of morality, but a matter of public health. The problems that have become so entrenched in our country, such as AIDS, illegitimate births, poverty, increasing crime and the breakdown of the nuclear family, can all be attributed to the debilitating effects of a public policy that condones sex without love or responsibility.

As research clearly indicates, America is not suffering from a lack of knowledge about sex, but an absence of values. Traditional values like love, commitment, responsibility, integrity and self control are still relevant today and must be taught.

The greatest threat to America's security is not foreign invasion, but destruction from within. As Samuel Adams, known as the "Father of the American Revolution," said, "A general dissolution of principles and manners will more surely overthrow the liberties of America than the whole force of the common enemy. While the people are virtuous they cannot be subdued; but when they lose their virtue they will be ready to surrender their liberties to the first external or internal invader. . . . If virtue and knowledge are diffused among the people, they will never be enslaved. This will be their great security.

Modern sex-education curricula has already been proven misguided and inadequate. How much more disease, death and social disintegration do we have to encounter before we return to time honored and tested principles? It's time for the message of sexual purity to be sounded in the United States once again. Concerned Women for America is calling upon all legislators, parents and educators to work together for renewal in the social, economic, and health spheres of American life by promoting abstinence throughout this nation.

Abstinence-Only Sex Education Programs Are Flawed

by Susan Flinn

About the author: *Susan Flinn writes for Advocates for Youth, an organization dedicated to creating programs and promoting policies that help young people make informed and responsible decisions about their sexual health.*

In 1996, Congress passed funding for an educational program to encourage sexual abstinence for all unmarried people. The entitlement provides $50 million annually through the Maternal and Child Health (MCH) Bureau and requires a sizable state match. The program will cost over a quarter of a billion dollars while promoting inaccurate and harmful messages about sexuality.

The definition of "abstinence-only" education conflicts with the concepts underlying effective sexuality and health education programs. The MCH programs must not discuss contraception or disease prevention. In contrast, effective programs include information about abstinence as well as contraception and sexually transmitted disease (STD) prevention.

Abstinence-only education is defined as an educational or motivational program which teaches:

- as its exclusive purpose, the social, psychological, and health gains to be realized by abstaining from sexual activity;
- abstinence from sexual activity outside marriage as the expected standard for all school-age children;
- that abstinence from sexual activity is the only certain way to avoid out-of-wedlock pregnancy, sexually transmitted diseases, and other associated health problems;
- that a mutually-faithful monogamous relationship in the context of marriage is the expected standard of human sexual activity;
- that sexual activity outside the context of marriage is likely to have harmful psychological and physical effects;
- that bearing children out of wedlock is likely to have harmful consequences

Reprinted from "Abstinence-Until-Marriage Education: Unrealistic and Irresponsible," by Susan Flinn, *Advocates for Youth,* February 1998. Reprinted with permission from *Advocates for Youth.*

for the child, the child's parents, and society
- young people how to reject sexual advances and how alcohol and drug use increase vulnerability to sexual advances; and
- the importance of attaining self-sufficiency before engaging in sexual activity.

Abstinence-Only Education Is Unrealistic and Ineffective

The language allows no flexibility for discussing disease and pregnancy prevention methods other than abstinence and fails to acknowledge the world in which most Americans live. Already, without a federal program providing inaccurate information, U.S. adolescent reproductive health indicators are dismal. The nation's teen birth rate is eight times higher than rates in comparable European nations. Nearly three million youth are infected with an STD, annually. AIDS is the sixth leading cause of death for youth aged 15–24 and, each year, nearly half of all new HIV infections occur in people under age 25.

This program lies to young people by telling them that all sexual activity outside marriage is harmful and that only abstinence will protect them. By age 20, 80 percent of males and over 75 percent of females have had sex. In an age of AIDS, and in a country where less than seven percent of men and 21 percent of women were virgins on their wedding night, such messages are unrealistic and dangerous.

"The . . . teen birth rate [in the United States] is eight times higher than rates in comparable European nations."

Compared to teens receiving balanced, realistic sexuality education, abstinence-only program participants are *more* likely to increase sexual activity and to have sex at younger ages. There is no link between balanced, realistic sexuality education and increased sexual activity among teens; the World Health Organization has concluded that this sexuality education neither increases sexual activity nor encourages young people to have sex at earlier ages.

A 1996 study which examined evaluations of abstinence-only programs discovered numerous flaws, "weak" research designs, and "simplistic and frequently inappropriate analyses." In some cases, statistical information "[made] it clear that the evaluator has a limited grasp of the appropriate inferences to be drawn from the data."

The authors conclude *they do not know of any "methodologically sound studies that demonstrate the effectiveness of curricula that teach abstinence as the only effective means of preventing teen pregnancy."* Many abstinence-only evaluators are nonetheless willing "to draw conclusions wholly unwarranted by the data" and claim the programs are effective.

Abstinence-only education is also unpopular. At least 80 percent of Americans consistently report they want sexuality education taught in public high schools. Almost 95 percent of Americans support AIDS prevention education; a similar percentage of parents support AIDS prevention education in schools.

Almost two-thirds of Americans think "Just Say No" campaigns are ineffective at preventing teenage sexual risk taking.

Experts Say Abstinence Does Not Work

Several well-respected organizations have made statements about this issue.

The National Institutes of Health maintains that abstinence-only education "is in direct conflict with science and ignores the overwhelming evidence that other programs would be effective. Such programs (abstinence-only) cannot be justified in the face of effective programs and given the fact that we face an international emergency in the AIDS epidemic."

According to M. Baldo, P. Aggleton, and G. Slutkin, "school programs which promoted both postponement and protected sex when sexually active, were more effective than those promoting abstinence alone. Sex and AIDS education do not promote earlier or increased sexual activity in young people. More positively, they may lead to an increased uptake of safer sex practices."

The Institute of Medicine argues that "lack of open communication and information regarding sexuality and STDs fosters misperceptions and may actually encourage high risk sexual behaviors. . . . All school districts in the United States should ensure that schools provide essential, age-appropriate STD related services, including health education."

New Programs Are Not Realistic

States are not required to accept these funds, but those which do must provide $3 for every $4 of federal funds. While some states allocate funds, others require a local match or that programs obtain their own matching funds.

The state match must be used only for abstinence-only programming, and cannot fund balanced, realistic programs or components. The restriction on using state money for more comprehensive programs makes it impossible for states to pay for the abstinence portion with MCH funds and the comprehensive portion with the state funds.

Applications for funding are considered based upon how well the proposals "meet the legislative priorities," including the eight components listed above. Although the programs are not required to place equal emphasis on each element of the definition, a project may not be inconsis-

> *"Compared to teens receiving balanced, realistic sexuality education, abstinence-only program participants are **more** likely to increase sexual activity."*

tent with any aspect of the abstinence-only definition. It is unclear how a program can teach factual and medically accurate messages *and* present nonmarital sexuality as being below the expected standard of human behavior and having harmful psychological and physical effects.

The definition was written specifically so that the funds would not be used for balanced, realistic education. Congressional staff, complaining that previous abstinence programs "included information about birth control thereby undermining the abstinence[-only] message," have stated that "no program that in any way endorses, supports, or encourages sex outside marriage can receive support from the abstinence[-only] money."

"Abstinence-only education 'is in direct conflict with science and ignores the overwhelming evidence that other programs would be effective.'"

In general, state public health agencies have crafted programs which will help support young people as they negotiate a path to adulthood. At the very least, state public health officials have attempted to fund programs which do not lie to, or otherwise harm, teenagers. Most state proposals target young people and concentrate on younger, rather than older, adolescents. Many require local control of the program and local financial match. Many states are conducting media campaigns, helping communities assess their own needs, and implementing mentoring or substance abuse programs. Some states are using the MCH money to supplement on-going programs.

National Coalition for Abstinence Education

Focus on the Family's National Coalition for Abstinence Education [NCAE] has issued "report cards" which give failing grades to most state proposals for not meeting the law's legislative priorities. State plans receive lower scores if they fail to target all teens under 19 (many plans concentrate their efforts on younger teenagers); do not equally stress all eight components of the law; use the majority of funds for education outside of the schools; or are not absolute about unmarried people remaining abstinent.

Plans were criticized if significant funding is used for media campaigns or for after-school, recreational, substance abuse prevention, or mentoring programs. States were also graded poorly if plans include referrals to comprehensive health care providers. If the plan uses terms like "fact-based, respectful, and culturally relevant," the program received a failing grade.

NCAE has also distributed a Pledge Card to those serving on the Advisory Committees overseeing the programs. This loyalty oath requires members to vote for proposals meeting all eight of the legislative components and including messages that nonmarital sex is wrong. It is unclear what NCAE intends for those who refuse to sign the pledge.

Next Steps for Abstinence-Until-Marriage Education

In order to generate the required state match, funding for family planning, comprehensive sexuality education, and AIDS prevention may decline. Additionally, programs that apply for abstinence-only funding will be hard pressed to explain opposition to increased financing of such programs in the future.

The abstinence-until-marriage education program should provide an opportunity to evaluate whether withholding reproductive information is an effective public health strategy. The programs are required to report information about the program's target populations and several performance measures addressing adolescent sexual activity. *None* of the required measures examine the program's goal of reducing out-of-wedlock sexual activity and childbearing in the general population.

The *performance measures* are: teen pregnancy rates (ages 15–17); percent of adolescents, 17 and younger, who have had sexual intercourse; the rate of teenagers (15–19) contracting a bacterial STD in the reporting period; and the birth rate for teenagers ages 15–17. The 1997 Budget Reconciliation Bill also included funding for evaluating abstinence-only programs. It is not yet clear what requirements will be attached to this funding.

Since most states are targeting youth ages 9–14, accurate evaluations will require a lengthy evaluation, following participants until they are at least 18. Furthermore, sexual activity and pregnancy rates are notoriously difficult to calculate; honest responses may be hard to obtain after participants are told it is immoral to experience either.

Since abstinence-only education was passed as an "entitlement," there are very few mechanisms for addressing the program. Essentially, the program will be automatically funded every year until the entitlement is repealed. Such a remedy appears unlikely in the current conservative political climate. The Christian Coalition's effort to target low-income and minority communities includes the goal of increasing funding for abstinence-only education "to provide for—at minimum—an additional $150 million in . . . funding per year."

Congressional supporters of realistic sexuality education and AIDS prevention will work to broaden the entitlement where possible, but real change may have to wait for a more progressive political environment.

Sex Education Can Prevent Teenage Pregnancy

by SIECUS

About the author: *The Sexuality Information and Education Council of the U.S. (SIECUS) is an organization that promotes comprehensive education about sexuality and advocates the right of individuals to make responsible sexual choices. SIECUS provides the guidelines for sex education for kindergarten through twelfth grade and publishes the report, "Facing Facts: Sexual Health for America's Adolescents."*

You would think a two-week trip to Europe would yield stories of picturesque walks through ancient towns and beautiful churches and conversations over a glass of wine or a great cup of coffee. Our stories do involve such things, but the real story behind our trip is not simply tourism.

The Euroteen Study

In 1985, the Alan Guttmacher Institute [an organization that works to protect and expand reproductive choices for all people] published the findings from their "Euroteen" study highlighting the different rates of teen pregnancy, births, and abortion in 37 developed countries.

To learn how some European countries yield their low rates of negative outcomes and high rates of positive outcomes from adolescent sexual behavior, Advocates for Youth [an organization that promotes policies which help young people make informed decisions about their sexual health] and the University of North Carolina at Charlotte organized a six-city study tour of three countries in July and August of 1998.

On July 25, 1998, 40 professionals and graduate students from the United States set out to learn about adolescent sexual behavior and responsibility from some of the people and places that report the greatest success—the residents of the Netherlands, France, and Germany.

From site visits and lectures, to panel discussions with health educators, youth workers, policy makers, AIDS activists and general practitioners, we have returned

Reprinted from "Report from a Study Tour: Teen Sexuality Education in the Netherlands, France, and Germany," by SIECUS, December 1, 1998. Reprinted with permission from SIECUS.

to the United States with a new view of the positive impact of access to sexuality education, public information, and medical services targeted to young people.

Sexuality Education Is Working

In the Netherlands, France, and Germany, adolescent sexuality is regarded as a health issue, rather than a political or religious one. An overwhelming majority of the people and institutions in these countries support sexual health. In all three countries, but most notably in the Netherlands, teens are educated about safer sex and have access to both birth control pills and condoms if they have sexual intercourse.

In a lecture given by Jany Rademakers, one of the premiere researchers on adolescent sexuality at the Netherlands Institute of Social Sexological Research (NISSO), we learned that the efforts toward education and access are working: 85 percent of Dutch teens use contraceptives at first intercourse; 46 percent report using condoms only, and 24 percent report using both a condom and birth control pills, known in the Netherlands as "Double Dutch." Birth control pills and condoms used together not only work to prevent pregnancy and sexually transmitted infections, but they also encourage both partners to take an active role in preventing infection and pregnancy.

In the countries studied, adolescents are valued, respected, and expected to act responsibly. Equally important, most adults trust adolescents to make responsible choices because they see young people as assets, rather than problems. That message is conveyed in the media, in school texts, and in health care settings.

> *"The reality is that teens in the Netherlands, France, and Germany have intercourse without as many negative consequences as teens in the United States."*

Consider these simple comparative facts. According to 1990–95 data from the United Nations Population Division, the teen birth rate per 1,000 girls 15 to 19 years old is 64 in the United States, 13 in Germany, 9 in France, and 7 in the Netherlands.

Teen abortion rates are also profoundly lower in Europe than in the United States. Comparative data compiled by Advocates for Youth shows that the abortion rate per 1,000 women 15 to 19 years old is 17 in the United States, 7.9 in France, and 5.2 in the Netherlands. (For Germany, the abortion rate is 8.7 for women ages 15 to 49.) Additionally, in the countries studied, teens begin having sexual relations more than one year later than American teens and have fewer sexual partners during their teen years than their American peers.

No Abstinence Education

The reality is that teens in the Netherlands, France, and Germany have intercourse without as many negative consequences as teens in the United States.

86

But European teens get something that American teens don't. They get inundated with positive messages aimed at helping them avoid unplanned pregnancy and sexually transmitted infections.

Most important, the messages sent to Dutch, German, and French teens are not designed to ask them to abstain from intercourse until marriage. In our visit to the Mouvement Francais pour le Planning Familial (MFPF), we asked the speaker, Monique Bellanger, director of the MFPF Documentation Center, if her organization promoted abstinence until marriage. Her response was to laugh and say, "We don't give such a message. It's bad for your health."

> *"[European] media are engaged in helping young people make healthy sexual choices, not simply titillating audiences with sexual content for the sake of . . . money."*

The impetus to provide access to contraception, condoms, and comprehensive sexuality education is based on the desire to further reduce abortions and sexually transmitted diseases. Sexuality education is not necessarily one "course" but is integrated throughout many subjects and grade levels. The focus of sexuality education is on normalizing sexuality in the context of adolescent development, assuring medical accuracy, promoting values of respect and responsibility, and encouraging communication in relationships.

In reviewing curricula at a site visit to the Catholic Pedagogical Center (a teacher training center in the Netherlands), we were struck by how much sexuality was taken for granted. At first glance, the curricula stumped us. We wondered where the sexuality education was. On closer inspection, and with the help of a translator, we found that nearly all the curricula included sexuality information within the context of life skills.

One chapter would explain how to do laundry. The next would explain contraception. School teachers also reported taking this comprehensive approach to heart by leading discussions and lessons on relationships and sexuality in literature classes while reading classics such as *Romeo and Juliet.*

Massive Public Education Campaigns

In Germany, there is a national sexuality education policy, but individual states can determine which curricula to use. In France, sexual health is promoted through national campaigns that encourage students to participate in safer sex and AIDS prevention poster contests. The winning posters then become an integral part of national media campaigns. In the Netherlands, schools distribute safer sex pamphlets just before the school holidays because officials know that many students will have sexual relationships while on vacation. Students in the Netherlands are also tested on national school exams for proficiency in sexuality education.

One of the key findings from our review of educational materials in all three countries about the various teaching approaches to sexuality was that professionals and educational materials honored the fact that sexuality exists for more than one week during one year in high school.

All three countries also have massive public education campaigns targeting safer sex behaviors and condom use. Media are engaged in helping young people make healthy sexual choices, not simply titillating audiences with sexual content for the sake of advertisers' money. Television, radio, billboards, tour buses, discos, pharmacies, post offices, and medical clinics

> *"[Europeans] worked collaboratively to create educational materials and provide access to services to address the negative outcomes."*

are all enlisted in the public education efforts. In the Netherlands, parents can pick up informational booklets on tips for talking to their children about sexuality from their local post office. One of France's safer sex media campaigns targeting young people during school breaks exclaims, "On Holiday I forget everything . . . except condoms!"

These countries also appear to have little concern that sexually explicit media messages will encourage young people to have intercourse. In fact, most of the school curricula for adolescents include some nudity, as do most television and print media campaigns. Humor also plays a big role in conveying messages of safer sex and responsibility. The bottom line for the European media approaches to sexuality is that accurate and factual information is used in accessible, realistic, and humorous ways to reach their audiences.

Non-Adversarial Cooperation

The mass media sexuality education campaigns are supported and encouraged by a broad array of people with an equally broad array of beliefs and values, ranging from AIDS educators and parents to religious leaders and policy makers. We in the United States can learn from this non-adversarial relationship between religious communities and advocates for sexuality education, and, as a result, should encourage all groups to make strides toward a place where young people and families are supported to be sexually healthy.

Religion and politics have little influence on policies related to adolescent sexuality in the European countries we visited. For example, the church in France doesn't involve itself in school sexuality education, contraceptive services, or safer sex messages in the media. And with multiple political parties in the Netherlands, no single candidate or party can polarize the electorate around adolescent sexual issues.

National health insurance in all three countries gives youth convenient access to sexual health care, including contraception and emergency contraception. In the Netherlands, a teen girl who wants to use a birth control pill does not need to have a medical exam, to complete any forms, or to give her real name at the clinic. A health professional interviews the young woman, conducts a health history screening, and barring any contraindications, the young woman will leave with free birth control pills.

All three countries provide youth-friendly access to sexual health care by having free or low-cost services, numerous locations with generous hours of operations, and social support for making responsible sexual choices. Most young people get contraceptives through their family physicians, and clinics run by MFPF in France, the Rutgers Stichting in the Netherlands, and Pro-Familia in Germany provide services as well.

European and American Families Are Similar

The tour yielded little new information about working with parents on family communication about sexuality. European studies about family sexuality education revealed dynamics similar to American families. In a study presented by Janita Ravesloot, a professor from Leiden University in the Netherlands, Dutch parents and teens expressed different impressions of the communication and education that happens at home regarding sexuality. This finding is similar to studies of parent-child communication in the United States.

Although European young people report receiving very little sexuality education at home, when asked specific questions about sexuality and sexual health, it becomes clear that young people are still successful in getting information about responsibility in relationships, where and how to get safer sex protection, and their family's values about sexuality.

Parents in the Netherlands may not directly teach their children everything they want to know about sex—a third of parents in the study view their adolescents' sexual lives as private. Dutch parents consider themselves "supportive from a distance" around their teens' sexual behaviors. They don't forbid sexual intercourse because they don't want their teens' experience to be like the parents'. They fear it may push their children to rebellion and risk. One parent we interviewed said, "I don't want my kids to be sneaky." Most parents don't set rigid rules—but they do want children to have serious, responsible, healthy relations. As in the United States, mothers do most of the communication with their children about sexual and relationship issues. Mothers negotiate with teens about their sex lives. Also, as in the States, parents say they've talked with their children about sex, while their children say they have not. Parents say they are "liberal" while their adolescents say they (their children) are restricted. Parents consider themselves liberal in comparison to their own upbringing. Only 1 percent of Dutch parents in the study insisted on abstinence for their adolescents.

In a German study, the findings were similar to the Dutch. Some of the specifics include the fact that 80 percent of the family communication about sexuality is introduced by the mothers, and that 40 percent of German young men report that they get no sexuality education from their parents. Findings from the same German study indicate that almost 60 percent of parents regard human sexual behavior as a natural part of their life and, as a result, German families are taking sexuality education far more seriously than earlier generations. The role of the family in sexuality education is profound, not simply as a prevention method, but as a model for building healthy relationship and communication skills.

Positive and Inclusive Sexuality Education

All three countries that we visited during the European Study Tour have one major thing in common. The positive and inclusive nationally funded sexuality education initiatives have all come about in the past 40 years. The Dutch, French, and Germans have made significant strides within the last two decades toward implementing national harm-reduction programs at their best. They saw the negative outcomes of HIV infection and too-early pregnancy, and worked collaboratively to create educational materials and provide access to services to address the negative outcomes, not by attempting to prevent sexual behaviors.

A portion of an interview journalist Bill Beckley had with artist Louise Bourgeois appeared in the September 1998 *Harper's Magazine*. The exchange that follows best sums up the contrasting social norms between European countries and the United States. The interview read:

Bill Beckley: You were born in France, but you lived a long time in the United States. What is the difference between the aesthetics of the two countries?

Louise Bourgeois: I'll tell you a story about my mother. When I was a little girl growing up in France, my mother worked sewing tapestries. Some of the tapestries were exported to America. The only problem was that many of the images of the tapestries were of naked people. My mother's job was to cut out the—what do you call it?

Beckley: The genitals?

Bourgeois: Yes, the genitals of the men and women, and replace these parts with pictures of flowers so they could be sold to Americans. My mother saved all the pictures of the genitals over the years, and one day she sewed them together as a quilt, and then she gave me the quilt. That's the difference between French and American aesthetics.

Reframing our society and culture while affecting beliefs and practices about adolescent sexual behavior in the United States will not be easy, but we have seen that it can be done.

We cannot ignore the fact that poverty, lack of hope for the future, and an inadequate public education are strong predictors for sexual risk taking. But we can help adolescents make responsible choices about sexuality.

Adolescents can make healthy decisions. We need to help build a context in which they are supported to feel good about themselves and their bodies, remain healthy, and build positive, equitable, loving relationships. Our European neighbors reminded us that sexuality can be a normal, healthy, and pleasurable aspect of being human—even for adolescents.

Sex Education Encourages Teenage Sex

by Tony Snow

About the author: *Tony Snow is a nationally syndicated columnist.*

Both political parties say education will top the list of priorities for the national elections in 2000. If so, here's the issue of the year: sex education.

Long ago, when public schools first thought of removing the "l" from their titles [pubic], religious organizations complained about carnal instruction. The press and the educational establishment quickly tarred these critics as hicks unwise to ethics in the age of birth control and warned that untutored adolescents would learn on their own about the birds and the bees.

Sex Education Encourages Sex

Little did anyone suspect that schools eventually would be the ones encouraging kids to rut with abandon—and that the federal government would dole out millions of bucks to subsidize what amounts to a Condom Cult.

The Centers for Disease Control [CDC] have begun cranking out "Programs That Work" manuals bearing such titles as "Be Proud! Be Responsible!" "Becoming a Responsible Teen" and "Reducing the Risk." The texts claim to aim at cutting down on pregnancy and sexually transmitted diseases, but they also adopt methods that would do any brainwasher proud.

Consider what cults do. First, they weaken family ties. The aforementioned programs require students to make written or spoken pledges of confidentiality: Youngsters are singled out for opprobrium if they tell their parents. Schools assiduously keep moms and dads in the dark.

Texts Humiliate Virgins

Cults also jangle moral codes by introducing new standards and reinforcing them through behavior modification. Here's an example from "Reducing the Risk": "(T)here are many ways to avoid pregnancy and sexually transmitted disease (STD). You could become a hermit who never talks to anyone or does

Reprinted from "Tax Dollars Support Sex-Education Outrage," by Tony Snow, *Conservative Chronicle,* October 27, 1999. Reprinted with permission from Creators Syndicate.

anything. Or, you could avoid pregnancy and STD by being so unpleasant that everyone stays clear of you. Or, you could never become involved in a romantic relationship." Translation: Only geeks, losers and dirtballs avoid teen sex.

A training manual tells teachers to humiliate students who believe in abstinence. It instructs them to 1) say, "Condom use is dealt with in Pastoral counseling of couples," 2) put the burden on the kids by asking, "How they want it handled if (other) students ask the questions" and 3) "Ask opponents to sit in on the group. *INSIST* they sit in on the group."

> *"Abstinence education is far more successful at reducing pregnancy and STDs than [sexuality education]."*

Another manual recommends role-playing to stress the importance of "protection." The case for deferred gratification is reduced to this: "We believe in abstinence; if we plan, we're *BAD!*" (Never mind that abstinence education is far more successful at reducing pregnancy and STDs than this bilge.) In keeping with the brainwashing theme, the text outlaws conscientious objection: "To (refuse role-playing) would run counter to the purpose of the group."

Cults also ensnare members by creating bizarre rites. That way, members not only share experiences, they also have incriminating evidence on one another.

Condom Cult

The Programs That Work establish an elaborate system of idiocies, the first of which is that high-schoolers, beginning at age 13, spend an inordinate amount of time fondling condoms. "Becoming a Responsible Teen" promotes having kids serve as "personal trainers" for each other—applauding dexterity with condoms and swapping suggestions about technique.

"Be Proud! Be Responsible!" invites youngsters to "brainstorm ways to increase spontaneity . . . store condoms under mattress, eroticize condom use with partner, use extra lubricant, use condoms as a method of foreplay, use different colors and types/textures . . . think up a sexual fantasy . . . hide them on your body and ask your partner to find it. . . ." It tells young lovers to have fun by purchasing condoms together.

Teachers behave like fools by speaking in slang, most of which is unprintable. To take one of the milder locutions, just imagine your old health teacher announcing in chirpy tones: "Class! Pay attention! Now we're going to talk about yodeling in the canyon!"

Finally comes the matter of discipline for would-be apostates. The CDC uses cash as a lure. Schools get big bucks to join the fun. If they balk, somebody else gets the loot. Meanwhile, as we have seen, educators treat skeptical students like lepers.

These programs, which have been, um, exposed by Ohio State Board of Education member Diana Fessler and *Cincinnati Enquirer* writer Linda Cagnetti, illustrate the way in which elites are using "public health" as an excuse for over-hauling everything from economic regulation to public instruction. Activists who argue with regard to abortion that government should stay out of the bed-room now want Uncle Sam to enter children's bedrooms.

I have left out the most outrageous stuff, but you get the idea: We finally have discovered something more obscene than the Starr Report [in which Indepen-dent Investigator Kenneth Starr reports on the sexual activities of President Bill Clinton] and it is a public-school curriculum supported by our tax dollars. This leads to the question: Why should any parent trust educators who willingly teach teens how to construct "dental dams" for oral sex?

Enforcing Statutory Rape Laws Can Help Prevent Teenage Pregnancy

by Michael W. Lynch

About the author: *Michael W. Lynch is the Washington editor for* Reason *magazine.*

"When I was growing up, there was a saying, 'Sixteen will get you 20,'" remembers Eloise Anderson, director of California's Department of Social Services. "Sixteen" is a girl's age; "20" is the number of years an adult male would spend in prison if he had sex with her. For years, statutory rape laws languished in disuse. But studies show that a significant proportion of teens are impregnated by adult men, prompting politicians to once again apply such laws, which remain on the books in all 50 states. At the federal level, the 1997 welfare-reform law called on states and localities to "aggressively enforce statutory rape laws."

Statutory Rape Convictions Cause Concern

In the Golden State [California], Governor Pete Wilson created a program to do just that. Since its start in 1995, California's Statutory Rape Vertical Prosecution Program, which provides grants to counties to prosecute statutory rape, has convicted more than 1,454 offenders, with 5,000 more under investigation. The program is netting few teenage lovers. According to Michael Carrington, who ran the program until recently, the typical scenario involves a 13-year-old mother and her 25-year-old male partner. Some counties won't even prosecute statutory rape cases unless there is a five-year age gap between partners. One such county is San Diego where, after a year and a half of prosecution, the average male offender is 25.7 years old; the average girl, 14.4 years.

Yet, in the Washington policy circles where teen pregnancy is studied, such programs have had a very cool reception. One reason for this is ideological.

Liberals instinctively dislike the idea of using criminal law to solve social problems. And conservatives fear that an overreaching state, fueled by exaggerated media reports, will prosecute people for victimless crimes. Meanwhile, so-called children's advocates amass data, reinterpret studies, and challenge the assumptions behind efforts to punish adults who impregnate young girls. They are campaigning to convince policy makers and the public that applying these rape laws won't reduce teen pregnancy. By such efforts, some valid assertions have been made, but also some statistical sleight of hand.

Young Fathers, Younger Mothers

Beginning in the mid 1980s, researchers began uncovering data that undermined the assumption behind teen sexuality programs, that teen pregnancies were the unintended consequences of sex between teenagers. In 1989, *Family Planning Perspectives*, the peer-reviewed journal of the Alan Guttmacher Institute which specializes in fertility issues, published an article that focused on the partners of teen mothers in Baltimore. While the article, "Fathers of Children Born to Young Urban Mothers," found that most partners of teen mothers were under 20, it did find evidence of an age gap. "On average, the fathers of all infants born to white teenage women were four years older than were the mothers, and those of infants born to black teenage mothers were 2–3 years older," the study reported. Such an age gap isn't shocking, considering that it is customary for women to date and marry slightly older men. But later research revealed that the two- to three-year average underestimated the age differences for the youngest girls.

In 1992 and 1993, U.C.-Irvine graduate student Mike Males published a series of studies in scholarly journals that showed significant age differences between these unwed, underage mothers and the fathers of their children. In 1996, an article in the *American Journal of Public Health*, "The Ages of Fathers in California Adolescent Births, 1993," pretty much shattered the assumption that teens were impregnating teens. Examining California data, Males and his colleague Kenneth Chew reported that "adult post-school men father two thirds of the infants born to school-age mothers and average 4.2 years older than the senior-high mothers and 6.7 years older than the junior-high mothers." More alarmingly, they found that the younger the girl, the wider the age gap. Roughly half of the babies born

> *"Roughly half of the babies born to 15-year-old mothers were fathered by adult men no longer in school."*

to 15-year-old mothers were fathered by adult men no longer in school. In addition, a 1995 article in *Family Planning Perspectives*, "How Old are U.S. Fathers?" found an average age gap of four years between mothers aged 15 to 17 and their partners.

Such data effectively refuted the notion that girls 15 and younger were pregnant because their male classmates didn't have easy access to condoms. Earlier studies showed that teenage mothers with much older partners are often victims of sexual assault as children. "The possibility that such early child-bearing represents an extension of rape or sexual abuse by male perpetrators averaging one to two decades older remains a serious question," Males and Chew wrote.

Playing Both Sides

The New York–based Alan Guttmacher Institute plays prominent roles on both sides of the debate over teen pregnancy. Its 1995 journal article, "How Old are U.S. Fathers?" which first noted the substantial age gap between teenage mothers and their partners, was written by two of its in-house researchers, David Landry and Jacqueline Darroch Forrest. "Half of the fathers of babies born to women aged 15–17 were 20 years of age or older," they wrote. "On average, 15–17 year-old mothers were four years younger than their baby's father." Landry and Forrest concluded that "the mean age difference shows generally that the younger the mother is, the greater the age difference between her and her partner." They warned that "this type of age difference suggests, at the least, very different levels of life experience and power, and brings into question issues of pressure and abuse." They also pointed out that since two-thirds of babies born to mothers aged 15 to 17 are fathered by adult men, "some of the assumptions underlying many of the programs and policies aimed at reducing teenage pregnancy and childbearing are not correct."

> *"21 percent of babies born to minor girls—an astonishing one in five—were fathered by men at least five years older than the mothers."*

Landry and Forrest's study was fact based, containing little of what can be interpreted as political spin. Yet looking back, it is clear that others at the Guttmacher Institute and their allies in the field of teen-pregnancy prevention originally welcomed these data as a justification for expanded government programs—programs that would provide outreach to these disenfranchised and misguided men who were impregnating young girls. What they got out of a Republican-dominated Congress and Republican-dominated statehouses, however, was stepped-up emphasis on putting such men in jail. Delaware, Florida, Georgia, and California recently revived efforts to enforce statutory rape laws. Lawmakers in other states, including Pennsylvania and Texas, are pushing proposals to do so.

It was the empirical findings on pregnant minors with older partners that reinvigorated statutory rape law enforcement. In order to arrest the states' rush to the courts, it became imperative for Landry and Forrest's colleagues at the Guttmacher Institute, and their political allies elsewhere, to discredit these statistics. In the spring of 1997, a group of Urban Institute researchers published an article in the Guttmacher Institute's *Family Planning Perspectives* to recast the data. In "Age Differences Between Minors Who Give Birth and Their Adult Partners," the authors, Laura Duberstein Lindberg, Freya L. Sonenstein, Leighton Ku, and Gladys Martinez, note that there is a big difference between a 19- or even an 18-year-old having a baby with a 20- or 21-year-old man and a 14-year-old having a baby with the same man.

> *"The youngest girls are most vulnerable to the predatory acts of older men."*

"While a 25-year-old man fathering a child with a 15-year-old would probably meet with social disapproval," Lindberg et al. argue, "the same might not be true for a couple consisting of a 21-year-old and an 18-year-old, particularly if they were married." They then note that women aged 18 to 19 account for nearly two-thirds of teen pregnancies (62 percent), and these pregnancies cannot be the result of statutory rape, even if the father was an adult. As a result, statutory rape laws can affect only a bit more than one-third of all teenage births. Of the remaining 38 percent, Lindberg et al. report that roughly 21 percent meet the definition for statutory rape, which is typically a minor girl at least five years younger than her partner.

Motherhood and the New Math

Lindberg and company's main empirical conclusion, which has been amplified in another study, is that "overall, among births to 15–19-year-olds in 1988, only 8% involved unmarried women aged 15–17 and men who were at least five years older." From this, the authors derive a major policy conclusion:

New state and federal initiatives that emphasize the vigorous enforcement of statutory rape laws are unlikely to be the magic bullet to reduce rates of adolescent childbearing, since the number of births that result from acts covered by such laws is small. Policymakers need to pay attention to broader means of reducing teenage childbearing, such as sexuality education, youth development and contraceptive services.

Even if the 8 percent figure is an accurate presentation of the problem, one appropriate question might still be, So what? "Why wouldn't we be concerned about just one child who was involved in this type of relationship?" asks California's Anderson, referring to the girls in the 15- to 17-year-old range. "It doesn't matter to us if there is one or a million. For us, the issue is that the guy is breaking the law, the mother is powerless, and the outcome of this relationship is detrimental to society."

But, in fact, the 8 percent finding misses the mark by a factor of nearly three. Lindberg et al. produced this low number by excluding the partners of mothers aged 18 to 19 from their calculations, on the reasonable ground that these men cannot be prosecuted for statutory rape. But then, they include these same 18- to 19-year-old women in the pool when calculating what percentage of babies born to teenage mothers have partners at least five years older. Thus 62 percent of the fathers are removed from the numerator while their partners are included in the denominator. "When it is convenient to put them in the equation to minimize the problem of older males, they put them in the equation," says U.C.-Irvine's Mike Males. "When it is inconvenient, they take them out. They have generated a soundbite figure, the 8 percent, that is the least justified, but they are making it the most prominent."

A More Honest Approach

A more honest approach would focus on the relevant group: mothers aged 17 and under. (Actually, since the age of consent is 16 in many states, girls under 16 would be the relevant pool. But the data, in their present form, are not aggregated in a way that would allow this analysis.) If you pull out all the adults, and even the married minors, Lindberg et al.'s data show that 21 percent of babies born to minor girls—an astonishing one in five—were fathered by men at least five years older than the mothers. Deviating little from the previous studies, Lindberg et al. also found that the "youngest mothers in the sample were the most likely to have a partner five or more years older." Four in 10 babies born to 15-year-old girls were fathered by a man who was at least 20 years old.

In June 1997, these findings made their way into a summary report released by the privately funded National Campaign to Prevent Teen Pregnancy, a Clinton-inspired effort to reduce teen pregnancy by one-third by 2005. The report, "Not Just For Girls: Involving Boys and Men in Teen Pregnancy Prevention," was written by Theodora Ooms, a researcher at the Family Impact Seminar, a Washington-based institute that examines family issues. Ooms's paper is based on a "roundtable meeting of scholars, practitioners, and policy officials" which sought to "get the facts straight about the age between teen girls and their male partners and to explore the lessons being learned from the growing number of efforts to target males in teen pregnancy prevention."

In the first section of her paper, Ooms summarizes the results of the studies outlined above. After detailing the stark findings of the earlier studies, she notes that sensational media reports, led by the *New York Times*, "created considerable public alarm and compelled some states and communities to launch initiatives to enforce statutory rape laws aggressively." Relying on Lindberg et al.'s findings, Ooms stresses that births to girls with much older partners constituted only 8 percent of all births to teenagers. "Put another way," she writes, lest the point be passed over, "the teen mothers who have so captured the public's attention—those under 18 who are unmarried and have a much older partner—constitute less than one in ten of all teen mothers."

> *"While intellectuals argue about root causes, most everyone else should be able to see the value in giving meaning back to the term 'jailbait.'"*

Chapter 3

Questions of Objectivity

Ooms's paper attracted little attention, since it merely repackaged old studies and reported on a meeting of unnamed scholars. But it was tied to the release of another study that reported new data. This study, "Partners, Predators, Peers, Protectors: Males and Teen Pregnancy," was also commissioned by the National Campaign to Prevent Teen Pregnancy. The co-authors were from Child Trends Inc., a Washington-based nonprofit that researches issues affecting children. They analyzed newly available data from the Department of Health and Human Services' 1995 National Survey of Family Growth, which collects information on pregnancy and childbearing. The study focused on the first sexual experience of teenage girls: Was it voluntary? How old was her partner? Was contraception used? The Child Trends study found that nearly two-thirds of the first sexual partners of teenage girls were within two years of the girl's age and that nearly three out of four couples were going steady at the time. Sixty-nine percent of girls welcomed their first sexual experience.

Strangely, for a study tied to the Ooms paper, the data paint a picture strikingly similar to the findings of the older studies, even though they deal with first sexual experience as opposed to pregnancy. As in the previous studies, the

> *"The same people who are willing to absolve men of their responsibility want to heap a larger burden on the pregnant girls."*

data diverge by age. The younger the girl, the less likely her partner would be sharing a school, much less a classroom, with her. The study reports that "only 18 percent of girls who were younger than 14 when they first had sex had a partner who was within a year of their age; this was the case for 37 percent of teens who were 14–15 years at first sex, and for more than half of teens who were 16 years or older." The data on which the study was based show that 35 percent of girls 15 or younger first had sex with a partner at least three years older. Nearly one in five 13-year-olds lost her virginity to a man at least five years her senior. In addition, the study found that the wider the age difference, the less likely the couple would use contraception (79 percent for same age and 66 percent for difference of five years).

Youngest Girls Are Most Vulnerable

The data from the Child Trends study confirmed that the youngest girls are most vulnerable to the predatory acts of older men. The larger the age gap, the more likely sex was unwanted by the girl. While 26 percent of girls who first had sex with someone of the same age reported it as unwanted, 37 percent of girls whose partner was five or more years older did. Nearly 40 percent of 13- and 14-year-old girls reported their first sexual experience as unwanted; for those who had sex younger than 13, more than 70 percent reported it as unwanted.

The Child Trends study clearly adds to our understanding of teenage sexual activity, but the decision to tie its release to Ooms's paper, in which the data merely spun previously released studies, raises questions of objectivity. A spokesman for the National Campaign to Prevent Teen Pregnancy which commissioned the paper, John Hutchins, says one of the "key goals" of the expert roundtable and Ooms's paper was to examine the issue of statutory rape. "We didn't see the release of these reports as being corrective of these other studies," he says. "We don't dispute what they say. We just wanted to tease out what they meant." But the data are sure to disappoint those who want to make the case that the problem of statutory rape is of minor significance. All available data consistently show that the younger the girl, the older the man. And since it is the youngest girls whom government has the greatest interest in protecting, attempts to muddy the issue with creative statistics run contrary to the realities of teenage pregnancy and the interests of the youngest teenage mothers.

> *"It is simply prudent, moral, and just to build barriers to adult sex with minor girls."*

Even the smallest number that can be produced—Ooms's "less than one in ten"—still begs the question: Why shouldn't we care about one in ten? In 1994, about 393,000 babies were born to unmarried women 19 and under. At 8 percent, more than 31,000 of these babies fall into Ooms's "less than one in ten" category. In that year alone, 12,000 babies were born to unmarried women under 15 years old. The data indicate that 40 percent of these babies are the result of unions with a significant age gap. That's 4,800 babies. What California's Anderson wants to know from those researchers who are questioning statutory rape laws is, "Would they sanction their daughter, who is 15, being impregnated by a guy who is 27? Or is this something that we sanction for other people's children?"

Unintended Consequences

Realizing that this battle will never be won by data alone, opponents of statutory rape enforcement are advancing other arguments. Chief among them is the contention that these unproven programs may generate unintended consequences, making them worse than doing nothing at all. The Guttmacher Institute's Patricia Donovan made this case in the January/February 1997 issue of *Family Planning Perspectives*. In "Can Statutory Rape Law Be Effective in Preventing Adolescent Pregnancy?" Donovan draws heavily on interviews with "law enforcement officials, reproductive health care providers, women's rights activists and policy analysts" to put forth what seems to be the prevailing liberal view of teen pregnancy, and of why statutory-rape laws will not work. As Michelle Oberman of the DePaul University Law School explains in Donovan's paper, "Adolescent child bearing is the result of an intricate web of factors, including limited opportunity, entrenched poverty, low self-esteem and many other issues that statutory rape laws do not address." Circumstances, not individual decisions, generate unfortunate outcomes. In this view, adult men who pursue intimate relationships with minor girls are not responsible for getting them pregnant.

But, while intellectuals argue about root causes, most everyone else should be able to see the value in giving meaning back to the term "jailbait." Donovan recognizes this, quoting California officials who predict that their program, in time, will deter offenders. But she is unconvinced: "The enforcement strategy is only likely to work if the men it targets—and their young partners—know that these relationships are illegal." Donovan then quotes law-enforcement officials who claim that "predators know they aren't supposed to have sex with someone underage." But for balance, she quotes pregnancy-clinic administrators who claim that "very few know the rules."

It may be true that many 25-year-olds don't know they aren't supposed to have sex with 14-year-olds. But this doesn't mean that they won't get the message after an acquaintance, or even an acquaintance of an acquaintance, winds up in jail. This is what Carla Grabert, deputy district attorney in California's Kern County, is discovering, after a year and a half of prosecuting men for statutory rape. "The first time I talked to teen dads on probation, only a few knew there were laws against sex with minors," recalls Grabert. "Now when I ask the boys, 100 percent raise their hands. The word is getting out."

In any event, Donovan's article tries to play both sides of the issue. One of the arguments she advances against the law-enforcement approach is that it would prevent young girls from seeking pregnancy services. This may well be the case in some circumstances, and it is certainly a concern worth addressing; it is probably the reason that no state has mandatory reporting by health providers. But this can only be the case if the girls know that the sex in which they are engaging is illegal. Thus Donovan's argument holds that 15-year-old girls will know relevant details of the laws to which their twenty-something sexual partners are oblivious.

Putting Loving Fathers in Jail

Yet another argument is that enforcement of these laws will put loving and supportive fathers in jail. The short answer to this objection is discretion by law enforcement. Each case need not be prosecuted, and, in questionable cases, juries might not convict. What's important to keep in mind is this: If we threw away all laws against sex between adult men and minor girls out of a misguided fear of jailing supposedly loving fathers, parents would be unable to protect their teenage daughters from the designs of older men.

Drawing a hard line and prosecuting every individual who crosses it would be no less detrimental. There will always be cases where families are supportive of the couple doing the right thing—getting married and raising the child. Researcher Mike Males—who can hardly be accused of being soft on the issue—

estimates that only 10 to 20 percent of prosecutable cases should be prosecuted. It is of course problematic to openly advocate that law-enforcement officials selectively enforce a law. Inconsistent enforcement undermines respect for the rule of law and leads to charges that prejudices based on race, class, or other inappropriate criteria are driving enforcement decisions. To minimize abuses of power, citizens must always monitor law enforcement.

The California program shows how such discretion can be used wisely. Prosecutors, who claim to work closely with social-service providers, say that the threat of prosecution is often used to ensure that the man does not simply abandon the young mother and his child. In fact, sentencing recommendations include "establishing paternity; paying support; and attending parenting classes." The program provides prosecutors with wide discretion, and the focus has been on cases with the largest age gaps.

Three Categories of Statutory Rape

The state's law has three categories of statutory rape. Any sex with a minor (under age 18) is a misdemeanor. If the minor is three years younger than the adult, the case can be handled as either a misdemeanor or a felony. In cases where the adult is at least 21, and the minor no older than 15, prosecutors still have discretion between misdemeanor and felony charges, but the felony charges carry longer sentencing guidelines of up to four years in prison.

For those made nervous when prosecutors are afforded excessive discretion, a highly publicized Wisconsin case offered no reassurance. There, an 18-year-old man who had impregnated his 15-year-old girlfriend—as a result of consensual sex—was tried and convicted as a sex offender even though he was planning to marry the girl. Those welcoming strictly drawn legal lines want to make it more difficult for zealous or ambitious prosecutors—who may, for example, be seeking higher conviction rates—to target men as rapists when they have pregnant girlfriends.

Such problems have yet to arise in California. As noted in Donovan's paper, Orange County social-service workers often recommend marriage as a viable alternative to statutory rape prosecution. While this is often controversial—as one might expect in the case of a 20-year-old marrying a 13-year-old—such flexibility undermines the argument that enforcement will, on balance, make matters worse for both the girl and her baby.

In Defense of Predators

Researchers like Donovan appear bent on proving to skeptics that these men are not social pariahs. They want to rehabilitate the "predatory male" in the public mind, to transform him from a victimizer to a man who is himself a victim of society. Lindberg et al.'s study concludes with a call for policy makers to eschew the stick in favor of the carrot. "The disincentives to have sex with minors, such as expanding the reach and increasing the penalties of statutory rape laws, have already been advanced," they note. "Improving access to economic opportunities and achievement for disadvantaged men may be an equally important avenue to try to discourage adult sexual involvement and childbearing with minors."

The same people who are willing to absolve men of their responsibility want to heap a larger burden on the pregnant girls. In her penultimate paragraph, Donovan writes that, according to pregnancy-service providers, "it is not uncommon for adolescent women to pursue adult men," noting that adult men are more likely than the girls' schoolmates to "have a job, a car and money to spend." Thus it is the girls who should be the focus of government opportunity programs. Donovan concludes that these girls continue to seek out older men until they "have access to good schools and jobs and develop a sense that their lives can improve." This may well be so. And while a district attorney may not take note of a 17-year-old pursuing a 20-year-old, the purpose of enforcing a statutory-rape law is to ensure that the same 20-year-old resists any attempts for affection by a 14-year-old. The purpose of the law is to make clear that it is the responsibility of the adult to act like one.

Donovan and Lindberg et al. also seek to rehabilitate the "predatory male" by showing that he is often an active participant in the young mother's life. As a proxy for the quality of the relationship, they look at cohabitation patterns. Lindberg et al. note that 35 percent of pregnant minors reported living with their partner during most of their pregnancy. Nearly half were living with their partner at the time they were interviewed for the study, which was as long as 30 months after the birth.

One problem with these data is that they don't distinguish 17-year-olds living with 22-year-olds from 15-year-olds living with 24-year-olds. More to the point, they say nothing about the circumstances under which the couples were living. The data say even less about the troubling issue of consent: Is a 14-year-old girl capable of living with a 22-year-old man in a consensual relationship?

Carla Grabert, the district attorney who runs the statutory rape program in California's Kern County, prosecuted a case that illustrates this problem. A local girl was living with a man 14 years her senior. Physical abuse caused her to lose her first child. At age 16, she was pregnant again. This time, she decided, things would be different. On the condition that she obey household rules, her family took her back in. She had the baby. The father was convicted of statutory rape and sentenced to two years. Happy to have escaped the relationship, she is now in college and speaking to other teenagers about her experience. This case is certainly not typical, either in age breakdown or sanguine outcome, but it illustrates an important point: Living together, in and of itself, does not prove that a minor mother and an adult man are in a mutually beneficial relationship.

Prudent, Moral, and Just

In the final analysis, opponents of statutory rape laws simply distrust using the criminal code as a form of social control, a view with a healthy tradition in

America. But some acts, such as theft, fraud, and violent aggression, strike the vast majority of Americans as inherently criminal and therefore worthy of criminal sanctions. Few people would place a consensual relationship between a 17-year-old girl and a 19-year-old boy in this category, and any laws that attempt to do so will surely languish in the same disuse that marked statutory rape legislation for many years. But nearly everyone would place a relationship between a 13-year-old girl and a 20-year-old man in the criminal category. Thus the debate is over where to draw the line and what to do once the line is drawn, not whether to draw it in the first place.

The other fear harbored by those who oppose enforcing statutory rape laws is that the new criminal focus will drain resources that could otherwise fund what they consider to be more humane social-outreach programs. But statutory rape and social programs are not mutually exclusive. Anderson says she would be happy to have a law that no longer needs to be enforced because a social program eradicated the problem. Proponents of expanded social programs for adult males who impregnate young girls should expend their energy making the case for these programs based on their own merits, rather than engaging in a futile effort to attack a public policy that has not yet been demonstrated either a success or a failure.

The critics are, no doubt, correct to point out that enforcing statutory rape laws will not fix America's problem of teen pregnancy and out-of-wedlock birth. But most Americans will still probably feel that statutory rape enforcement makes sense. It is simply prudent, moral, and just to build barriers to adult sex with minor girls.

Enforcing Statutory Rape Laws Will Not Prevent Teenage Pregnancy

by Patricia Donovan

About the author: *Patricia Donovan is a contributing editor for* Family Planning Perspectives *and senior associate for law and public policy at the Alan Guttmacher Institute in Washington, D.C.*

Studies indicate that at least half of all babies born to minor women are fathered by adult men. In addition, there is a widespread perception that these young mothers account for the large increase in welfare caseloads over the last 25 years. As a result, a growing number of policymakers are embracing the notion that adolescent pregnancy rates can be lowered and welfare costs reduced if states more rigorously enforce statutory rape laws prohibiting sexual intercourse between adults and minors.

A New Focus on Statutory Rape

In 1996, several states have taken steps to punish men who violate these laws. Meanwhile, the new federal welfare law urges that "states and local jurisdictions . . . aggressively enforce statutory rape laws" and requires state welfare plans to outline an education and training program for law enforcement officials, counselors and educators that focuses on "the problem of statutory rape." It also directs the attorney general to implement a program to study the connection between statutory rape and adolescent pregnancy, with particular attention to "predatory older men."

Concerns about statutory rape are particularly acute in regard to the youngest adolescents. Although relatively small proportions of 13–14-year-olds have had intercourse,* those who become sexually active at an early age are espe-

---

*Seven percent of adolescent females have had intercourse by age 13, 13% have done so by age 14 and 19% have had intercourse by age 15.

cially likely to have experienced coercive sex: Seventy-four percent of women who had intercourse before age 14 and 60% of those who had sex before age 15 report having had a forced sexual experience. As policymakers and the public have become increasingly aware that the sexual partners of minor adolescent women are often not adolescents themselves but men 3–6 years older, concern has grown that protective measures, in the form of increasing enforcement of statutory rape laws, are necessary to guard these young women from abuse and exploitation.

The new focus on statutory rape laws, which have been on the books in every state for decades but have been largely ignored, has prompted public debate over the effectiveness of this approach as a potential remedy for the ongoing problem of adolescent pregnancy and childbearing. Advocates of tougher enforcement assert that adult men who "prey" on minor women will avoid these involvements if they believe that prosecution and severe punishment will follow violation of the law. The result, these advocates predict, will be fewer adolescent pregnancies and births, and, therefore, lower state and federal expenditures for welfare and health care benefits.

Enforcement Will Not Reduce Teen Pregnancy

Most experts, however, do not believe that greater enforcement of statutory rape laws can significantly reduce adolescent pregnancy and birth rates. As DePaul University associate law professor Michelle Oberman observes, statutory rape laws are probably necessary because "minor girls are . . . uniquely vulnerable to coercion and exploitation in their sexual decision-making." At the same time, she notes, "drawing a connection between enforcing these laws and lowering adolescent pregnancy rates flies in the face of everything we know about why girls get pregnant and why they choose to continue their pregnancies. The problem is much more complicated than simply older men preying on younger women." As Oberman and others observe, adolescent child-bearing is the result of an intricate web of factors, including limited opportunity, entrenched poverty, low self-esteem and many other issues that statutory rape laws do not address.

Interviews conducted with law enforcement officials, reproductive health care providers, women's rights activists and policy analysts in the summer and fall of 1996 found advocates of tougher enforcement of statutory rape laws suggesting that such an approach is a worthwhile strategy to consider, even if it turns

> *"Most experts . . . do not believe that greater enforcement of statutory rape laws can significantly reduce adolescent pregnancy and birth rates."*

out to have little or no effect on adolescent pregnancy and birth rates. Others warned that a concerted effort to prosecute statutory rape cases could in fact have an adverse impact. Many providers, for example, cautioned that such efforts could discourage some teenagers from obtaining reproductive health care, for fear that disclosing information about their partners could lead to a statutory rape charge and the man's incarceration. Moreover, statutory rape prosecutions could jeopardize the support that young mothers receive from their partners, and could make it less likely that these men would develop relationships with their children.

History of Statutory Rape Laws

Statutory rape laws are based on the premise that until a person reaches a certain age, that individual is legally incapable of consenting to sexual intercourse. Statutory rape was codified into English law more than 700 years ago, when it became illegal "to ravish," with or without her consent, a "maiden" under the age of 12. In 1576, the age of consent was lowered to 10.

Statutory rape laws became part of the American legal system through English common law. As in England, early lawmakers in this country adopted 10 as the age of consent. However, during the 19th century, states gradually raised the age of consent, in some cases to 21. Today, the age of consent ranges from 14 to 18 years of age; in more than half of the states, the age of consent is 16.

"The young women involved [in statutory rape cases] are often unreliable, hostile witnesses who change or deny their story on the witness stand."

While all states prohibit sexual activity between adults and minors in at least some circumstances, the laws vary enormously from state to state. Most statutes do not refer specifically to statutory rape; instead, they use designations such as sexual abuse, sexual assault, unlawful sexual conduct or carnal knowledge to identify prohibited activity. Most states have classifications and degrees of criminal behavior based on the age of the victim and the age difference between the victim and the "perpetrator."

The Law Is Rarely Enforced

Until recently, statutory rape laws applied exclusively to females, reflecting the long-held view that only girls and young women were so vulnerable as to warrant special protection. Today, however, most laws are gender neutral. Statutory rape laws were originally intended to protect the chastity of young women, and even today, many states allow defendants to argue that a minor who is already sexually experienced does not merit the protection of statutory rape laws. A few states also permit a defendant to claim that he or she mistakenly believed that the minor was older than was actually the case.

Statutory rape law is an area in which "the law on the books . . . differs markedly from the law in action." For example, data from the period 1975–1978 (gathered for a case argued before the Supreme Court) indicate that, on average, only 413 men were arrested annually for statutory rape in California, even though 50,000 pregnancies occurred among underage women in 1976 alone.

A major reason for the dearth of cases is that statutory rape is difficult to prosecute. The young women involved are often unreliable, hostile witnesses who change or deny their story on the witness stand. "They don't want to go into court and talk about sex," observes Kathleen Sylvester, vice president of the Progressive Policy Institute, which is cosponsoring with the American Bar Association a major study of states' enforcement of statutory rape laws.

A New Approach

California has begun a concerted effort to use its statutory rape laws as a means of reducing pregnancies and births among minors. The attempt was prompted by 1996 research indicating that two-thirds of babies born to school-aged mothers in the state were fathered by adult men, who, on average, were more than four years older than their adolescent partners.

"One of the most disturbing things about [the] exploding [rate of] teen pregnancy is that so many of the fathers are . . . men, 26 and 28 years old, having sex with 14-year-old girls," declared California Gov. Pete Wilson. "We've got to enforce statutory rape laws."

> *"[Health care] providers are especially worried that publicity about statutory rape prosecutions will discourage pregnant . . . adolescents from seeking medical care."*

In fall 1995, Governor Wilson announced a plan allocating $2.4 million of the state's adolescent pregnancy prevention funds to support prosecution of statutory rape cases. The plan, known as the Statutory Rape Vertical Prosecution Program, provides funding to hire additional personnel to work exclusively on statutory rape cases and allows the same prosecutor and investigator to remain on a case from beginning to end. According to Governor Wilson, vertical prosecution leads to higher conviction rates by fostering cooperation from victims and witnesses (who get to know the prosecutors) and permitting close communication between attorneys and law enforcement officials. The Governor predicted that "the increased ability to more aggressively prosecute statutory rape offenders will send a loud message that there will be serious consequences for adult men who impregnate minors, thereby creating a significant deterrent effect."

Initially, the 16 California counties with the highest rates of adolescent pregnancy involving adult men each received $150,000 to hire new staff. Early in 1996, however, the governor proposed a $6 million expansion of the initiative—bringing the total allocated to $8.4 million—to fund the state's remaining counties.

In addition to increased criminal prosecution, statutory rape offenders in California also face civil penalties under legislation enacted in September 1996. The "Teenage Pregnancy Prevention Act of 1995" provides for liabilities ranging from $2,000–$25,000, depending on the difference in the partners' ages. The statute claims that "illicit sexual activity between adult males and teenage . . . girls" has resulted in the state having the country's highest adolescent pregnancy and birth rates and spending billions of dollars annually to provide welfare and health care benefits to families headed by adolescents.

Several other states have also moved to identify and punish "male predators," the term often used by politicians and the media to describe adult men who have sex with minors. Delaware, for example, enacted the "Sexual Predator Act of 1996,"

> *"An overwhelming majority of young women who become pregnant and give birth are from poor or low-income families . . . [and] many see little reason to avoid pregnancy."*

which doubles the penalty for adults convicted of having sex with adolescents who are 10 or more years younger than themselves and increases the sentence for adults who have intercourse with minors younger than 14. "We will be investigating and prosecuting these abuse cases to the fullest extent possible," declared Governor Thomas Carper.

Delaware has also begun stationing state police in high schools to identify students who have become involved with adult men. "If we are committed to ensuring that our welfare reform and teen pregnancy prevention efforts are successful, we must recognize that older men frequently prey on young, vulnerable girls," the governor said. "Those officers have strong ties to the students and to the community, making them valuable allies in the effort to identify and investigate cases where girls are being victimized by adult men."

Meanwhile, Georgia raised its age of consent from 14 to 16 and increased to 10 years the minimum prison sentence for men aged 21 and older convicted of statutory rape. Florida voted in 1996 to make impregnation of a minor younger than age 16 by a male aged 21 or older a reportable form of child abuse. It also toughened its statutory rape law to prohibit sexual intercourse between a person aged 24 or older and a minor aged 16 or 17. (The law formerly stated that it was illegal for anyone to have sex with a person "of previous chaste character" younger than 18.)

"The specific problem we are trying to attack is older men preying on younger girls," explained State Senator Locke Burt, a cosponsor of the measure. Legislators in other states, including Pennsylvania and Texas, are also considering options for discouraging sexual activity between adolescent women and adult men.

The Deterrent Effect

Some advocates of more diligent enforcement of statutory rape laws believe that incarceration of men who are convicted of the crime will by itself have an impact on teenage pregnancy and birth rates. "We hope to remove from the streets many

of these men, a number of whom are multiple offenders," says Michael Carrington, deputy director of California's Office of Criminal Justice Planning, which ad-
ministers the vertical prosecution program. "To the degree that they are out of the
picture, the potential for adolescent pregnancy will be reduced."

A more common view is that adult men will be deterred from getting involved with minor women in the first place if a state makes clear its intention to
vigorously prosecute statutory rape and follows through on that threat with
some highly publicized cases. "When we prosecute a few of these guys, we
think it'll make a lot of guys think twice," predicts Jim Hollman, deputy district
attorney in California's Tulare County.

Garrett Randall, deputy district attorney in San Diego County, who has prosecuted more than two dozen cases and has won 19 convictions as of January 1,
1997, says that it is already happening in his area. "The idea that sex with
young females is against the law and the law is being enforced is spreading
here," he reports. (In 1997, Randall's office is prosecuting only cases in which
a pregnancy has occurred and the man is at least six years older than the underage woman.)

Unaware of the Law

The enforcement strategy is only likely to act as a deterrent, however, if the
men it targets—and their young partners—know that these relationships are illegal. Indeed, law enforcement officials and health care providers have different
perceptions of the public's knowledge of the issue. "Predators know they are
not supposed to have sex with someone who is underage," asserts Rick Trunfio,
an assistant district attorney in Syracuse, New York.

"The perpetrators know," agrees Carrington of California's Office of Criminal
Justice Planning. "They may not know all the legal definitions and precise sen-
tences for different age ranges, but they know they have been able to get away
with a crime."

In contrast, reproductive health care providers say that clients and their partners often know little or nothing about statutory rape. "Very few know the
rules," reports Margie Fites Siegle, executive director of the Los Angeles Re-
gional Family Planning Council. According to Sylvia Ivy, executive director of
The Help Everyone (THE) Clinic in Los Angeles, "Patients don't use terms like
statutory rape, or even rape, to describe sexual relationships that to others might
sound like rape."

Making Matters Worse

Law enforcement officials appear to see no harm in implementing a strategy
whose effectiveness is unknown. According to San Diego prosecutor Randall,
lack of evidence that enforcing statutory rape laws will lower adolescent pregnancy rates is "not a good reason not to try it."

In contrast, many reproductive health care providers believe there are good reasons not to pursue this strategy. Such an approach could exacerbate more problems than it would solve; providers are especially worried that publicity about statutory rape prosecutions will discourage pregnant and sexually active adolescents from seeking medical care for fear of having to reveal the identity and age of their partners. "I'm concerned that we'll have a situation in which women will not be comfortable disclosing information to their health care provider," says Siegle.

Providers point out that a young woman might be unlikely to jeopardize a relationship with a man whom she loves or from whom she receives support. Furthermore, they note, an adolescent might fear physical abuse in retribution for reporting a man to authorities. Teenagers are likely "to shut down" in such situations, says Amy Coen, executive director of the Planned Parenthood Association [a national organization that provides information about sexuality and reproduction] of the Chicago Area. "They won't seek help or, if they do, they won't tell the truth." In either case, Coen adds, "you cut off an avenue of [emotional] support."

Providers also point out that in some cultures it is accepted, even encouraged, for young girls to have relationships with much older men. Indeed, a family may promise their young daughter to a much older man, in part because he will help support the entire family. These cultural practices are "not going to change by throwing people in jail," observes Catherine Wiley, family planning director of the John Wesley Community Health Institute, a large community-based health center in Los Angeles. California officials acknowledge that cultural sensitivities are an issue in some circumstances, but say that taxpayers should not have to pay for these practices in the form of welfare and health benefits for adolescent mothers and their children fathered by adult men.

Health Care Providers as Police Officers

No state currently requires reproductive health care providers to gather and report information on the identity and age of their adolescent clients' sexual partners (unless they have reason to suspect a young woman has been abused). Providers say they do not routinely collect such information. "Trust is an important part of our relationship with patients," notes Ivy of THE Clinic. "If adolescents are communicating honestly with us about a partner and it turns out that he is an adult, a requirement to report the relationship as statutory rape would place clinics in a very awkward position; we would be used by law enforcement officials for goals they've determined to be in the public's interest, but which may not be in the patient's best interest. We want to be law-abiding, but we don't want to turn ourselves into an arm of the law."

Peggy Romberg, executive director of the Texas Family Planning Association, shares Ivy's concerns: "Mandatory reporting would place family planning providers in a terrible bind. We don't want the reputation that we're not a safe haven for counseling and services." On the other hand, she adds, clinics cannot afford to have employees arrested for failure to report suspected cases of statutory rape.

Such concerns are reflected in the Florida legislature's decision to exempt certain providers from a reporting requirement in the state's recently enacted law on child abuse. It requires that "known or suspected child abuse involving impregnation of a child under 16 years of age by a person 21 years of age or older . . . [be reported] immediately to the appropriate county sheriff's office or other appropriate law enforcement agency." The requirements do not apply, though, to "health care professionals or other persons who provide medical or counseling services to pregnant children when such reporting would interfere with the provision of medical services." One of the bill's sponsors acknowledges that at least some supporters did not want health care professionals "to turn into police officers."

Men as Felons, Not Fathers

Sponsors of programs designed to encourage men's involvement with their partners and children are also concerned about the consequences of mandatory reporting. Having to identify program participants who are adult men known to be involved with underage mothers would hamper their ability to enlist men into their programs. "There is a lot of concern about being put in a situation of having to report dads or would-be dads with adolescent partners," reports Jane Boggess, chief of California's office of family planning.

Advocates of more stringent enforcement of statutory rape laws have apparently ignored the philosophical conflict between these laws and existing statutes authorizing minors to consent to various types of reproductive health care, such as contraceptive services, screening and treatment for sexually transmitted diseases (STDs) and prenatal care. In Georgia, for example, where the legislature recently raised the age of consent for sexual intercourse to 16, state law authorizes minors to consent to STD testing and treatment, but some health officials have suggested that a statutory rape investigation be initiated whenever an underage female seeks STD services.

Such a policy, says state epidemiologist Kathleen Toomey, would "not only discourage kids from seeking care, undermining many of our prevention efforts, but it would deter providers from reporting cases, making it even harder for us to obtain reliable data on STDs."

The Father's Role

Supporters of tougher enforcement of statutory rape laws rarely acknowledge that such a policy may jeopardize relationships between adolescent mothers and their partners, and between these men and their children. These advocates frequently portray the men they seek to prosecute as irresponsible and predatory, interested in pursuing relationships with adolescents solely to engage in sex with minors. While this may accurately describe some individuals, other adult men who father the children of adolescent women play an important role in the lives of their offspring. Professionals who work with pregnant and parenting adolescents report that young mothers often receive crucial support in the form of cash, baby products and household goods from their baby's father.

"Adult [men] impregnating teenage girls is a troublesome phenomenon that is . . . unacceptable, . . . but we have to be very careful here," warns Lois Salisbury, executive director of Children Now, an advocacy group in Oakland, California. "We're talking about someone who has a baby to raise, and she needs resources to help raise that baby and she needs a father to help raise that baby. I don't see where it's human logic or nature that would motivate her to send that father to jail."

Coen, of Chicago Planned Parenthood, agrees. "Nobody is talking about the baby. If these young women are going to have these babies, I would like them to have some support in their lives."

Andrew Doniger, director of the Monroe County Health Department in New York (which has put up more than 100 billboards warning men that it is a crime to have sex with women younger than 17), adds that "if we drive a wedge between the father and the mother, it could make things worse for the youngsters."

In fact, the support of these adult men can be so important that welfare case workers in at least one California county have on several occasions recommended—and the courts have agreed—that an underage pregnant adolescent marry her adult partner (including a 13-year-old whose partner was 20). "We do this in those few cases in which it seems best for the girl and the child," explains Larry M. Leaman, director of the Orange County Social Services Agency. These are "cases where we have a man who is standing by the teenage mother, wanting to do the right thing, ready for a family, willing to support it and where the girl's parents, if they are around, also favor the marriage." (The agency's willingness to recommend marriage is highly controversial, and Leaman has ordered a review of the agency's handling of these cases.)

Rape Laws Are Not the Answer

The strict enforcement of statutory rape laws is the latest in a series of punitive measures that states have adopted recently in an attempt to force people to change their sexual and reproductive behavior. There has been considerable doubt as to whether other such proposals (e.g., the so-called family cap, which denies additional cash benefits to women who bear children while on welfare) will achieve their stated objectives—lower birthrates among women likely to require public assistance and reduced welfare caseloads and costs. Likewise, there is widespread skepticism as to whether the use of statutory rape laws will have a noticeable effect on adolescent pregnancy and birth rates or on the number of young women who have sexual relationships with adult men.

One has only to look at the statistics from California to understand these doubts. In the first 11 months of the state's vertical prosecution program, 617 statutory rape cases were filed statewide, of which 293 resulted in convictions. (Others are still pending.) While these numbers will surely rise in the wake of the program's recent expansion, the program is almost certain to address only a tiny fraction of the potential cases. In 1993 alone, for example, it is estimated that more than 30,000 underage adolescents in the state gave birth to a baby fathered by an adult man. Even Carrington of the Office of Criminal Justice Planning concedes that the impact of the vertical prosecution program will be "small, given the resources applied, compared with the gravity of the problem."

Michael Males, a University of California researcher, documented the extent of adult male involvement in births among California adolescents. He and other observers believe that the current focus on statutory rape reflects the frustration of politicians searching for "a simple solution" to the continuing problem of adolescent pregnancy and childbearing, rather than concern for the well-being of young adolescents.

"People are so eager to blame one cause so the situation can be fixed, "comments Mary Margaret Wilson, who is with the New York Council on Adolescent Pregnancy. "I'm scared people are going to say, 'Aha! This is why there is adolescent pregnancy. If we just get teens to name the perpetrators and their ages, the problem will go away.' People don't want to look at bigger things like poverty and racism."

Indeed, an overwhelming majority of young women who become pregnant and give birth are from poor or low-income families. Most lack access to good schools, face poor prospects for finding jobs and have little chance of marriage. As a result, many see little reason to avoid pregnancy and to postpone childbearing.

Moreover, while public debate over the use of statutory rape laws to prevent adolescent pregnancies has been framed largely in terms of so-called predatory older men who seek out young girls, the data suggest that these relationships account for only a slight fraction of adolescent births. In California, for example, fewer than 3% of all teenage births are to women younger than 15 (median age for this group is approximately 14.5); of these, nearly two-thirds are fathered by men 19 or younger. Among adolescent mothers aged 15–17 whose partner is an adult male, the women's median age is 17.1, while that of their partner is 21.4.

Additionally, providers say that it is not uncommon for adolescent women to pursue adult men. Adult men are more likely than adolescents to have a job, a car and money to spend. The accoutrements that adult men can provide "are an appealing beacon in the dark" for disadvantaged adolescents, observes Wilson. That is not likely to change until young women have access to good schools and jobs and develop a sense that their lives can improve.

"I think politicians have it backwards," concludes Valerie Small Navarro, a lobbyist for the California Civil Liberties Union. "They think you can slap a criminal penalty on the problem and the problem will go away." To reduce adolescent pregnancies, Navarro contends, "they have to be willing to invest time and money in women, not incarcerate men."

Chapter 4

What Alternatives to Parenting Exist for Pregnant Teens?

Chapter Preface

Teenage girls who learn that they are pregnant are faced with a difficult decision. Some girls decide to give birth to their babies and raise them. For those who choose not to become mothers, however, their legal options include abortion or adoption.

Abortion has been legal in the United States since the U.S. Supreme Court's 1973 landmark decision, *Roe v. Wade,* and has been the subject of heated argument ever since. Advocates of abortion argue that a woman has the right to control what happens to her own body. Proponents of abortion are especially strong advocates of abortion in the case of rape or incest, or when the mother is too young to care for the child. Advocates for Youth, an organization that works to reduce teenage pregnancy, argues that "teen mothers are less likely to complete their education, and more likely to have limited careers and . . . more likely to be poor." Abortion is a reasonable option for pregnant teens, defenders contend.

Those who oppose abortion argue that the fetus is a human being with a fundamental right to life. Therefore, they maintain, abortion is murder and immoral. Some opponents make exceptions for women or teens who became pregnant as a result of rape or incest. Others believe it is always wrong to put the desires of the mother over the life of the unborn child. Abortion critics contend that teens who obtain abortions will suffer regret and guilt their entire lives. David C. Reardon, director of the Elliot Institute, an organization that provides research and education on post-abortion issues, contends that after an abortion, women can experience "self-condemnation, lower self-esteem, difficulty with relationships, substance abuse, career problems, a cycle of repeat abortions, and more."

The decision about what to do about an unintended pregnancy is a difficult one. Should the pregnant teen decide not to become a mother, she may opt to have the baby and give it up for adoption. Or, she might decide to have an abortion. She might even choose to conceal the pregnancy and kill the newborn. The authors in the following chapter examine some of the alternatives to parenting chosen by pregnant teens.

Abortion Is a Beneficial Alternative to Teenage Parenting

by Krista Reuber

About the author: *Krista Reuber has a master's degree in public health and has worked with several nonprofit organizations to improve the health of women and children.*

My mother suspected I was pregnant even before I did. She noticed that I was run-down and tired, vomiting frequently and even more moody than my usual teenage state. As I was getting ready for school, she asked me if I might be pregnant. I was surprised and doubtful of her diagnosis, but I admitted that I had been sexually active for six months.

My mother always stressed the importance of communication and urged me to be open with her. When I was 12, we attended mother/daughter human sexuality seminars. Although she did not condone becoming sexually active at a young age, I knew that she wanted me to protect myself if I did choose to have sex. My boyfriend and I made an effort to use birth control, but we had unprotected sex several times.

My mother offered to bring my urine sample to a women's health clinic in Hartford while I was at school in our nearby suburban town. She learned later that day that my test results were positive and called me with the news at my after-school job at a shoe store. Positive . . . pregnant . . . me?! Even with my symptoms, I could not believe this was happening. I worked that afternoon in a state of shock.

Pregnancy Means Lost Opportunities

When I got home, my mother met me at the door with a hug and suggested that we discuss my options with my boyfriend at dinner the next evening. My parents stressed all the lost opportunities I would have; early motherhood would mean postponing my plans for college, putting my career on hold, restricting my travel, and placing a strain on me financially. My boyfriend, who was planning to attend a prestigious university on an athletic scholarship, echoed those sentiments. He felt that neither of us was ready to accept the responsibilities of parenthood. They all made it clear, however, that it was my decision and that they would support me no matter what I chose.

From an analytical standpoint, all of this made sense. I knew that I wasn't ready for motherhood. Still, I longed to know what the experience was all about. How would it feel to have my body change so dramatically? What would the baby look like? What would it be like to have someone so dependent on me? After several days of emotional turmoil, I gained some clarity. I decided that it would not be fair to bring a child into the world if I was not ready to care for it in all the ways that it needed and deserved. Terminating the pregnancy was the right thing for me to do at the time.

Harassed by Protestors

My mother and boyfriend accompanied me to the clinic for the abortion. As we entered the parking lot we saw a crowd of about 60 men and women holding signs and pamphlets. I was concerned. I had heard about anti-choice groups picketing and bombing women's health clinics. My mother glanced about nervously and told me not to worry—but obviously something was wrong.

I was afraid to get out of the car. When I finally did, a group rushed at me and began shouting, 'Don't do it—don't kill your baby!' and 'You'll regret this for the rest of your life!' My boyfriend used his 6'4" stature to push my mother and me through the swarming crowd and toward the clinic entrance. As I neared the door, a slight man with thinning white hair grabbed my arm and in a raspy voice begged me not to go inside. Terrified, I looked at my boyfriend and noticed his clenched jaw. In one quick motion, he freed me from the man's hold and hurried us through the door.

I was safe, but an emotional wreck. I could see silhouettes of the protestors through the sheer curtains—arms flailing, signs bobbing—and I could hear their muffled chants. My eyes filled with tears—tears of fear and anger. How dare they harass me! How dare they grab me! The decision had been hard enough without this. My mother hugged me and told me how sorry she was about the mob outside. The clinic staff also apologized, but conceded that there was little they could do to make them go away.

> *"Early motherhood would mean postponing my plans for college, putting my career on hold, restricting my travel, and placing a strain on me financially."*

By now I was sobbing, and I felt weak and shaky. Fortunately, the stack of forms I had to fill out and the counseling session that I had to attend gave me something else to focus on, and I regained my composure.

A Woman's Right to Choose

The physician who performed the procedure was very nice and apologized about the protestors. He made every effort to comfort me, promising that I would be fine and that later in life when I was ready to have children, I would have a wonderful family.

By the time we left more than three hours later, the protestors had gone. I was so drained that I fell asleep in the car and did not wake up until the next morning. During the days that followed, I grew increasingly enraged at the audacity of the protestors. I believe that the woman—and no one else—has the right to make decisions about her life and health. There is no excuse for the hostile, intimidating behaviors that anti-choice protestors direct toward women seeking abortions. No one should have to go through what I did.

My experience had a profound impact on my life, from my political views to my career choice. Today, I have an unwavering commitment to women's reproductive health care, and I am proudly pro-choice.

Abortion Is Harmful to Teenagers

by Colleen

About the author: *Colleen participated in a case study examining the effects of the abortion she had in 1983 when she was eighteen.*

I was 18 and dating a man my parents strongly disapproved of. So they "made a deal" with me: they would send me to college if I would break up with him. I agreed, though I never really meant to keep my end of the bargain.

Pushed to Have an Abortion

I realized I was pregnant when the smells from chemistry class kept making me sick. A friend convinced me to go to her doctor in town. He diagnosed pregnancy immediately, saying, "Such a shame, another young one." He told me not to worry, that "it" could be "taken care of." He never once said anything about keeping the baby, but gave me a card from the local abortuary.

Although I had no strong religious convictions, the visit to the clinic for my initial "consultation" left me feeling bad. The nurse told me to come back in a week with the money to have it done.

I had heard some things about abortion, and I knew it was probably wrong. So that whole week, I talked with friends and teachers, looking for advice. One female teacher in particular advised me to have it done. She told me that she had had several abortions, that it was "nothing," and that I didn't need this trouble in my life right now.

No one, at any time, told me anything about adoption or keeping the child. In fact, one of my teachers was a nun—and I approached her, too, with my problem. I think now that I really wanted someone to say "No! Don't do it!" But even the nun told me that abortion was the best route for me.

My boyfriend didn't have the money, so my parents volunteered to pay for it. When I broke down in front of them, saying that I thought it was wrong to do this, they told me they would *kick* me out of the house if I didn't have the abortion. My father said he wouldn't have any "little brown babies in his house!"

Reprinted from "Looking for Advice in All the Wrong Places," by Colleen, *Post-Abortion Review,* Fall 1993. Reprinted with permission.

(My boyfriend was Italian–Puerto Rican.) They told me that if I had the baby, I would be completely on my own. I felt like there was absolutely no way I could escape the inevitable.

The Abortion Procedure

When the time came, my boyfriend and some friends from school went with me. There were no protesters, no pro-life people. In fact, during the whole time of this crisis, I never heard a word about or from the pro-life side.

I was led to a room with a whole group of girls, just like me, waiting to have their babies killed. No one talked. No one looked at anyone else. They called our names, one by one.

I was very scared, mostly of the pain they said I might feel. With the counselor, I mostly cried. But she just agreed with everyone I had talked to. Yes, this is a bad time to have a child. Yes, you're too young. Yes, having a child costs a lot of money. Yes, it would be so hard for you to raise a child on your own. Yes, this is the best thing to do.

Waiting to have my name called, I tried to convince myself of these things. I just wanted the whole thing to be over with.

> *"The abortion wrecked my life. Emotionally, I was a different person before and after it. It left a path of destruction in my life."*

Finally they called me in and put me on a table. The dilation was extremely painful. A counselor held my hand and told me not to cry, it would be over soon.

The suction machine was very loud—a horrible noise. They had a picture on the ceiling for you to look at so you wouldn't have to think about what was happening to you. The image of that picture is burned into my memory. They took my baby from me while I looked at people walking in the rain.

Abortion Does Not Solve Problems

My boyfriend got drunk while I was in the clinic. He could hardly drive me home. He was late picking me up and I stood on the corner in front of the clinic, bleeding and embarrassed until he came.

When we got back to my dorm room, I was crying. I told everyone how awful it was, and how I wished I hadn't done it after all. My boyfriend laughed at me—laughed at me!—and said, "Well, that's what you get for screwing around!" One of the guys from school tried to throw him out, and they got into a fight. It was a horrible scene. I'm sure he got drunk to try and deal with it; he knew, deep down, that it was wrong. He was only trying to blame me for it so the responsibility for it wouldn't weigh on his shoulders.

In the end, the abortion did not "solve all my problems" as everyone had promised. My parents still kicked me out. I had to quit school. I married the boyfriend. It didn't work out. He became an alcoholic and a drug addict. He beat me up and brought other women into our bed.

One night during a drunken spree, he held a knife to my chest. I told him to kill me, that I wanted to die. I had nothing. No parents, no husband, really, no baby, and no self-respect. How *could* he respect me? I had killed our child. How could I look at myself in the mirror every day? I was a murderer. I truly wanted to die. Soon after this, we were separated and divorced.

Guilt and Pain

My abortion was about ten years ago. To me, it's like a bad, bad nightmare, deep in the past, best forgotten. I still haven't told anyone in my present life (my husband, my church friends, anyone I respect) about the abortion. I can't. I know that they would see me differently, and I couldn't stand that.

I've had one child since then, and I'm pregnant again. These children are my joy—and my forgiveness from God. My little boy is so, so precious and wonderful. If I had only known how sweet and wonderful a baby is, I never would have done it—not in 2 million years.

I now picket the clinics in the area, and I write letters to the paper and give money to pro-life groups. This helps a little—I feel that I need to do *at least* this much.

It's obvious that the abortion wrecked my life. Emotionally, I was a different person before and after it. It left a path of destruction in my life. My family, my first marriage, my image of myself—all a total wreck. Nothing will ever be the same.

I know now the lies I was told, the truths that were withheld from me, the facts that were glossed over or left out. As a pregnant woman, I go to my doctor's office and see pictures of babies in tummies. Month by month, I hear my baby's heartbeat. I'm told how to do everything that's best for my baby's health. Why is it legal across town to *not* tell these things?

I am just glad that I'm able to tell others. I'm glad that I can be outside that clinic when no one was there for me. I may not be able to confess my abortion, but I can *fight* abortion!

Adoption Is a Beneficial Alternative to Teenage Parenting

by K. Mahler

About the author: *K. Mahler is an associate editor for* Family Planning Perspectives.

Adolescent mothers who place their newborns for adoption are more likely than those who rear their infants to experience regret over their decision one year after the birth. However, according to a study of pregnant and postpartum teenagers in Ohio, these reactions are not associated with higher levels of depression or diminished feelings of efficacy. Moreover, adolescents who choose adoption complete more education, have higher rates of employment and lower rates of welfare receipt, and engage in less sexual risk-taking than do teenagers who keep their infants.

A Study to Gauge Adoption's Benefits

Researchers interviewed 181 adolescents at three public health clinics, two crisis counseling centers and one private social service agency in urban Ohio between October 1987 and December 1992, when the young women were pregnant or had recently delivered a baby. Follow-up interviews were conducted at birth and at six, 12 and 24 months postpartum. The study sample included 113 teenagers who completed all follow-up interviews: 87 who had kept their babies and 26 who had placed their infants for adoption.

At the first interview, the researchers collected a range of demographic and socioeconomic data. The adolescent's parenting decision was determined by the legal status of the child six months after birth.

The 12- and 24-month follow-up surveys examined the adolescent's satisfaction with her parenting decision. Questions addressed feelings of regret (scored on a four-point scale, with 1 representing least regret), the belief that the decision was the "right thing to do" (measured on a four-point scale, with 1 indicating "definitely not") and whether the teenager would recommend her course of action to a peer in a similar situation. The follow-up surveys also measured depression, perceived control over implementing plans, employment status, family receipt of Aid to Families with Dependent Children (AFDC) and sexual risk-taking (i.e., whether the young woman continued to engage in sexual intercourse and, if so, her frequency of contraceptive use).

At baseline, the adolescents ranged in age from 12 to 19, with a mean age of 17. Two-thirds of the study participants were white, 60% were attending school and 92% were unmarried. Fifty-eight percent of the participants lived in families receiving AFDC, and 23% held at least part-time jobs. The majority of participants reported the pregnancy as their first, although 10% indicated it was at least their third.

Teens Who Choose Adoption Feel Normal Sadness

In a number of respects, teenagers who kept their newborns were significantly different from those who placed their infants for adoption. At the initial interview, they were older (17.4 years vs. 16.7 years), less likely to be attending school and more likely to be living in a household receiving AFDC support. They also were less likely to have lived with both parents at age 10 and had somewhat less educated mothers.

At both 12 and 24 months after giving birth, the adolescents as a group were largely satisfied with their parenting decision. The mean regret score for the entire sample was 1.6 at both follow-up points, and the "right decision" score for the two surveys was 3.8-3.9. In each survey, approximately 60% of the young women indicated that they would recommend their decision to other pregnant teenagers.

Results of a correlational analysis, in which teenagers who had kept their infants were scored 0 and those who had placed their newborns for adoption were scored 1, indicated that one year after giving birth, an adolescent's parenting decision was positively associated with feelings of regret and negatively associated with the belief that she had made the right choice. The strength of these relationships lessened by 24 months postpartum, although the correlation between parenting decision and feelings of regret remained significant.

> *"According to socioeconomic indicators, adolescents who had placed their infants for adoption were significantly better off than were young women who had kept their children."*

In analyses controlling for baseline differences between the two groups of adolescents, the researchers found that two years after the young women gave birth, their levels of satisfaction with their parenting decision differed little. Those who had placed their newborns for adoption were significantly more likely than were those who had kept their babies to regret their decision. The two groups were equally likely to believe they had made the right decision and to report that they would advise other pregnant adolescents to make the same choice. Moreover, they did not differ in their levels of depression or feelings of efficacy: Both groups of young women reported moderate levels of sadness at the 12- and 24-month follow-ups, and adolescents who had kept their infants were as likely as those who had placed them for adoption to feel a sense of control over their lives.

Teens Who Choose Adoption Are Better Off

However, according to socioeconomic indicators, adolescents who had placed their infants for adoption were significantly better off than were young women who had kept their children. At 24 months postpartum, teenagers who had chosen adoption had completed more years of education, had a higher rate of employment (61% vs. 28%) and had a lower rate of AFDC receipt (33% vs. 75%). In addition, teenagers who had placed their babies were less likely to engage in risky sexual behavior than were adolescents who had kept their babies.

The researchers hypothesized that the enhanced socioeconomic circumstances of adolescents who had chosen adoption would somewhat ease the regret they experienced over their parenting decision. They tested this supposition by examining the differences in the relationship between a young woman's parenting decision and her level of satisfaction with that decision before and after socioeconomic variables were entered into hierarchical regression equations. For all three measures of satisfaction, the change in the coefficients suggested support for their assumption: One year after a birth, the socioeconomic benefits of having chosen adoption were associated with small increases in a teenager's satisfaction with her parenting decision. Similar findings were not apparent, however, at 24 months postpartum.

The investigators used a similar method to examine changes in satisfaction as a consequence of decreased sexual risk-taking. The benefits of engaging in less risky sexual behavior appeared to modestly increase the probability that a young woman would recommend her decision to a peer. However, in all other respects, changes in sexual behavior had little impact on an adolescent mother's satisfaction with her parenting decision.

In conclusion, the researchers note that the sadness a young woman experiences following a decision to place her child for adoption is part of a natural process and is not associated with long-term psychological distress. Nonetheless, they emphasize that professionals working with adolescents who have chosen adoption must be aware of the loss such a decision entails. However, the investigators also stress that the choice to place a child for adoption has significant advantages for adolescent mothers; these benefits, they suggest, should be explained clearly to pregnant teenagers so they are better equipped to make a well-informed parenting decision.

Most Pregnant Teenagers Do Not Choose Adoption

by Kristin Luker

About the author: *Kristin Luker is a professor of sociology at the University of California at Berkeley.*

Advocates for adoption as a solution to childbearing among unwed teens ignore a number of inconvenient facts. For example, most infertile couples seeking to adopt are white, and most of them wish to adopt only healthy white newborns. (An estimated half-million children are living in foster care, but there is little political pressure to make these children available for adoption, because they are the wrong color, the wrong age, and the wrong class.) But white teenage mothers—who in 1992 accounted for about 60 percent of teens giving birth out of wedlock—are more likely than black teenage mothers to marry after the birth of a child and to be living with the father of their baby at the time of the birth, making them unlikely candidates to relinquish their children. Thus, if more women gave up their children for adoption, there would simply be more children in foster care, since many of them would be black and the adoption market for such children is limited.

Fewer Teens Choose Adoption Today

Throughout the past half-century, unwed pregnant women were encouraged to enter a maternity home, have their baby, give the baby up, and return to life as unmarried women. At least, this was the preferred option for white women. As early as 1935, observers were confident that black extended families would be able and willing to accept out-of-wedlock children, although it is not clear whether such families would be acting out of preference or making a virtue of necessity; until the mid-1960s, most homes for unwed mothers refused to accept blacks. Today it is much less common for an out-of-wedlock child, of any race, to be given up for adoption. Whereas just thirty years ago the single, never-married mother was something of an oddity, now women of all ages are choosing to live as single mothers. In the 1965–1972 period, about 20 percent of white babies and 2 percent of black babies were relinquished for adoption; in 1973–1988, the proportions fell to 8 percent and .2 percent, respectively; and in 1982–1988, the figures were 3 percent and 1 percent. Even among unmarried mothers younger than seventeen, only about 8 percent of infants are given up for adoption.

These figures are only estimates because nowadays a substantial number of adoptions are arranged privately between the birth mother and the adopting couple, without the intervention of any state or federal agency. Often a lawyer assists in the process, but he or she is a private agent working for individual clients. The national adoption tracking system was disbanded in 1975, but Christine Bachrach has estimated that in 1982 more than 90 percent of all unmarried teenage mothers kept their children, and that even in 1971, before abortion was legalized nationally, more than 70 percent of white teenage mothers and 90 percent of black teenage mothers kept their children. Here, as in so many areas of sexual and reproductive behavior, the patterns among white and black teens are becoming increasingly similar.

The limited data we have also suggest that those young women who do give their children up for adoption resemble young women who have abortions more than they resemble young women who choose to rear their children. They are more affluent, have higher aspirations for themselves, and are performing better in school.

> *"Today it is much less common for an out-of-wedlock child, of any race, to be given up for adoption."*

Early motherhood is still not the first choice of young women who see themselves as having options. Since abortion is now legal and single mothers are no longer stigmatized, young women must actively choose whether or not to become mothers. Thus, although there are still young women who become pregnant out of wedlock and who do not wish to get an abortion or to be a mother (that is, women who are candidates for giving a child up for adoption), their numbers are relatively small, and dwindling. For many young women, choosing to continue a pregnancy means choosing to raise a child. Today the decision to keep a child is one that tends to be made before the baby is born, and unless abortion is recriminalized this situation is unlikely to change.

Valuing Money over Love

Still another barrier to using adoption as a way of solving the problem of early childbearing is the fact that the moral landscape has changed in the past three decades. People now think about adoption and its meaning in very different ways. Regardless of their opinions and decisions on the adoption issue, young mothers can be heard using moral language to talk about their choices:

127

> I know I can't keep my baby. I can't give it all the things a baby needs and I
> sure can't dump it on my parents because they can't afford to take care of their
> own family. I've decided to give it up for adoption. I think it's better for the
> baby to give it up to parents who can't have a baby themselves. I think that
> I'm really doing a favor to my baby, although I'm always going to wonder
> what it looks like and what it's doing. (Christina, seventeen, white, Colorado)

This traditional position is becoming rarer these days, and was never very common among minority mothers, who knew that their children would have a difficult time finding adoptive homes. More common is the view of adoption expressed by this young mother:

> Sure I thought about it, but I could never do it. I know a lot of people could do
> a better job than me of being a mother and they can't get pregnant, but that's
> not my fault. I'm not going to go through nine months and then give someone
> else the benefit. (White sixteen-year-old, living in rural New England)

This skepticism is enhanced by the fact that since single mothers are no longer vilified by society, giving up the baby has come to seem dictated only by material considerations, as the young mother above suggests. Young women believe they can love their children and can gauge the depth and commitment of their love, whereas the love of adoptive parents is an unknown quantity (and in recent years media reports of adoptive parents who abuse or even kill their children have given a special edge to this concern). So for many young women the only argument in favor of adoption is that their baby will have a better material life. In its starkest aspect, adoption means placing more value on cold hard cash than on a young woman's capacity to love.

> *"In its starkest aspect, adoption means placing more value on cold hard cash than on a young woman's capacity to love."*

Adoption Is Not Seen as the Moral Choice

Recent discussions focusing on adopted children who have sought reunions with their biological mothers raise another question—namely, the ways in which adoption may be harmful to children:

> I think as the kids got older it might be harder on them, because they would
> think, "Well, why didn't my mom want me? Was it because she just didn't
> want me, or because she couldn't support me, or . . .?" There's always going
> to be that time of depression. (Kimberly, white, Colorado)

In view of the new options that have come to characterize pregnancy and parenting in recent years, asking an unmarried teenage mother to consider giving up her child for adoption is no longer as simple and morally correct as it once was. Whereas for earlier generations (especially white teens) giving up a child for adoption was thought to be in the best interests of the child and something that every mother who really loved her child would seriously consider, today the moral discourse surrounding adoption has shifted. For many young women these days, both white and black, the sentiments that traditionally surrounded adoption in the black community have more resonance: adoption is giving away your own flesh and blood; it breaks the ties between generations; and there is no guarantee that some stranger can and will love your child as much as you will, or at least as much as you imagine you will. Also, adoption means placing more value on money than love, while deprecating the one thing that poor and discouraged teens can value in themselves: a capacity for maternal love. Oddly enough, the conservative dream of "family values" plays itself out in perhaps its purest form among unwed teenage mothers in poor communities. These young mothers express a commitment to moral values over material advancement, a passionate attachment to children, and a willingness to try to sustain a family (albeit a nontraditional one) whatever the social and financial cost. As a result, policies aimed at facilitating adoption may be praiseworthy and valuable in their own right, but are largely beside the point as strategies to reduce the rates of pregnancy and childbearing among teenagers. Since they will do little to alter the options confronting young women, they will have correspondingly little effect on teenagers' behavior.

Chapter 5

Should Society Approve of Teenage Parenting?

Chapter Preface

In the United States at the end of the twentieth century, 32 percent of all babies were born to unwed mothers. Unmarried mothers are not stigmatized as they were twenty years ago when teen girls gave birth in secret, however. In fact, out-of-wedlock childbearing has been popularized by unwed celebrity mothers such as Jodie Foster and Rosie O'Donnell. In U.S. high schools, pregnant girls can become cheerleaders and members of the student council. Some high schools even offer day care for student-mothers.

Many analysts argue that society's acceptance of out-of-wedlock childbearing has encouraged more teens to become parents without getting married. They claim that such acceptance leads to more of the social and economic problems that they attribute to teenage pregnancy. Teenage mothers who bear children out-of-wedlock rarely continue with their education, they contend, and end up on welfare. Many commentators maintain that the children of unwed teen mothers suffer greater problems than do other children. A study conducted by the U.S. Department of Health and Human Services concluded that "except for the very highest income level, children raised in single-parent households are materially worse off, irrespective of race. They are worse off in terms of educational achievement, social well-being, aggressiveness, and difficulty with the law." Many researchers argue that in order to prevent these individual and social costs, society should stop sanctioning unwed motherhood.

Other experts argue, however, that stigmatization of unwed mothers creates a double standard; because societal disapprobation does not fall on the fathers of children born out of wedlock, shaming is unfair to girls. Martha Ezzard, a member of the *Atlanta Journal and Constitution* editorial board, argues that those who favor punitive approaches to teen childbearing "find it is easy to blame young girls for cultural ills that only adults can cure." Indeed, many argue that the high rate of out-of-wedlock childbearing among teens is a symptom of larger social problems like poverty and racism. These analysts maintain that the best way to help pregnant teens is to offer them financial and social support through community programs. Such programs, like Crittenton Homes—which offers young mothers a supportive place to live while they raise their babies—can help teen mothers become good parents and productive members of society.

Society's response to teenage parenting is a reflection of its values. Along with society's increased acceptance of premarital sex, there has been more acceptance of teenage childbearing. Because society's sanction can be a strong influence on individual behavior, the debate about early childrearing is a heated one. The authors in the following viewpoints argue whether or not society should sanction teenage parenting.

Criticizing Teen Mothers Is Unfair

by Mike A. Males

About the author: *Mike A. Males is a reporter on youth issues for* In These Times *magazine.*

Are children of teenage mothers more abused? More likely to be born with low birth weights or other defects? Less likely to do well in school? More likely to be hoodlums. . . .

The Mother's Age Is Not a Problem

What 99 percent of the comparisons of the children of teenage moms versus the children of adult mothers accomplish is further proof that yes, the progeny of poorer nonwhites indeed do less well in American schools and society than do that of wealthier whites. Yes, kids raised by parents with backgrounds of sexual and violent abuse tend to have more chaotic upbringings than kids whose parents were not abused. In none of this does the age of the mother in and of itself show up as the crucial factor.

Carolyn Makinson of Princeton's Office of Population Research reviewed several dozen studies from the U.S. and four other Western nations and found "remarkably similar" results:

> The most recent evidence indicates that the bulk of the adverse consequences of teenage childbearing may be of social and economic origin, rather than attributable to the effects of young age per se. . . . Some evidence indicates that if maternal age has an effect, it is only among very young teenage mothers.

An analysis E.M. Kinard and L.V. Klerman report that: of 7,100 U.S. children and their parents indeed found a small association between the child's intellectual development and maternal age—but concluded that the age of the mother was not the cause.

> The effects of parental age are apparently not biologic, but instead are due chiefly to the impact of sociodemographic factors and the tendency for young

mothers, especially blacks, to be overrepresented in lower socioeconomic groups and in female-headed households.

Teens and Low Birth Weights

In particular, teenage mothers are accused of producing babies with low birth weights, which in turn is the biggest predictor of poor infant health and development. Yet national vital statistics reports show the true cause of low birth-weight babies is economic disadvantage, reflected in race (Table 1).

Table 1: Poverty, Not Maternal Age, Is the Biggest Factor in Unhealthy Babies

Age of mother	Median birth weight[*]		Percent low birth weight[*]	
	White	Black	White	Black
10–14	3,240	3,080	10.3%	15.7%
15–19	3,310	3,130	7.5	13.5
20–24	3,380	3,170	5.8	12.3
25–29	3,440	3,190	5.1	13.1
30–34	3,460	3,190	5.3	13.4
35–39	3,460	3,200	6.3	15.3
40–44	3,450	3,200	7.0	15.1
45–49	3,410	3,220	10.0	15.5
All ages	3,410	3,170	5.1%	13.3%

[*]In grams. Low birth weight is less than 2,500 grams (5.5 pounds).

Source: National Center for Health Statistics (1995). *Vital statistics of the United States 1990. Volume I, Natality.* Washington, DC: U.S. Department of Health and Human Services, Table 1-104.

The greater poverty of blacks and their lesser access to prenatal care has devastating effects on infant health. So much so that a white teenager—even a white junior high-age mother—is much less likely to have a low birth weight baby than a black adult at every age level. A black mother age 25–29, for example, is 40 percent more likely to bear a low birth weight baby than a white 15 year-old. Black infants weigh half a pound less at birth than white infants. Note also that there is little difference between black teens and black adults in the birth weights of their babies. The lesser effect of young maternal age on birth weights is explained by the fact that younger mothers, regardless of race, are more likely to be poor than older ones. Except for mothers younger than 15 and older than 40, the pattern reflects economic status, not the age or race of the mother.

Teens and Depression

Another study by Makinson, which controlled for economic backgrounds still found a small relationship between mothers' ages and child development. The most important relationship was with mothers' scores on psychological tests of "malaise." Since a history of sexual abuse and rape is closely linked both to teen motherhood and malaise, this may also be a key factor. The federally funded 1992 National Women's Study found that rape victims (60 percent of whom reported being raped before age 18) are three times more likely to report major depression, four times more likely to have contemplated suicide, six times more likely to have developed post-traumatic stress syndrome, and 13 times more likely to have attempted suicide.

> *"There appears no health or child-rearing disadvantage related to the teen age of the mother except when the mother is very young (14 or younger)."*

Common declarations that teenage motherhood is a "disaster" or a "calamity" or entails "tremendous social and financial costs" evade confronting the real issue: The devastating effects of persistent inequality imposed on nonwhite races and economic disadvantage imposed on the young. Makinson puts the issue more formally:

> Symptoms of social and economic inequality may be more visible than the inequalities themselves, and are probably more easily, if less fruitfully, eradicated. Many of the adverse consequences of teenage fertility are symptoms of this kind.

Attacking Teen Mothers Is Unfair

In other words, attacking "teen mothers" is a politically facile substitute for genuine efforts to eliminate racial and economic injustice—particularly that foisted on the young. There appears no health or child-rearing disadvantage related to the teen age of the mother except when the mother is very young (14 or younger). On the other hand, a history of poverty and abuse appear to be crucial factors. As Makinson points out:

> To the extent that young age is an intermediate variable between adverse consequences and root causes that are of social and economic origin, postponing childbearing until the risks are no higher than average might mean postponing childbearing permanently for many women who will remain socially and economically disadvantaged.

That would be fine with conservatives such as Charles Murray, vocal in his *Bell Curve* argument that childbearing by low-income mothers, mostly nonwhite, is (to use the 1920s term his book resurrected) "dysgenic." Liberals who ascribe dire disadvantages to teenage motherhood, which is a surrogate for low-income motherhood, are making the same argument as Murray's without being as candid. If the parents are poor, there is no good age, no healthy age, no age at which "social costs" will not result from childbearing. Having a baby young disrupts schooling; having a baby old disrupts job and career.

Unwed Teen Mothers Who Excel Academically Should Be Admired

by Saundra Smokes

About the author: *Saundra Smokes writes for the* Syracuse Herald-Journal.

When I heard the news that one of my favorite teen-agers was pregnant, I got sick to my stomach.

For days, I turned the thing over in my head. The girl was book- and life-smart. At times, she seemed older and wiser, deeper than some of her peers.

I just knew she would end up at the head of line, leading her classmates in some kind of youth revolution that would benefit her school, her community, her generation. But she was pregnant and I knew she knew better.

What Might Have Been

I heard her speak it from her own lips that she had plans for the future and they didn't include being a teen-age mother.

Now she was on her way to motherhood, and I don't recall the girl ever having a steady boyfriend.

My anguish and nausea was prompted by the thought that what might have been had been sabotaged by what might be: a dream deferred or even defeated.

I have not seen her since I heard her news. I know when I do, I will hug her and try not to look at her protruding belly with sadness.

My insides might be churning. I might feel like screaming. But I won't push this girl away, make her feel as though she has committed the sin of sins, one that has caused her to be placed in a category different from her peers.

That is why I so agree with the decision of U.S. District Judge William Bertelsman, who ruled that two Kentucky teen-agers who had gotten pregnant could not be excluded from the National Honor Society.

The teens, Somer Chipman, 17, and Chasity Glass, 18, were the only two of

Reprinted from "Moms-to-Be Belong in High School Honor Society," by Saundra Smokes, *Denver Post*, January 6, 1999. Reprinted with permission from United Feature Syndicate, Inc.

33 eligible students at Grant County High School in Williamstown, Kentucky, who were not allowed to join the honor society. Chipman had an average of 3.9 out of 4.0, and Glass had an average of 3.7 out of 4.0.

The American Civil Liberties Union had filed a lawsuit on behalf of the girls, charging sexual discrimination.

The local honor society, which chooses candidates for the national group, had said that "the public interest requires support of the public schools' efforts to encourage high morals and strong character as part of the educational process," according to an Associated Press report.

The judge disagreed. He said the rights of the girls outweighed such a legal argument.

Let me be clear. I do not think we ought to applaud teen-age pregnancy.

I think schools ought to be pushing abstinence and religious institutions ought to be preaching the Bible, even if it is not popular or cool to tell teens they shouldn't be having sex.

And I am thrilled that teen pregnancy rates are down in general and significantly lower among African-American girls.

Pregnancy rates for them have declined 21 percent between 1991 and 1996.

> *"Any teen-ager, especially a pregnant one, who can maintain honor-society-level grades should be applauded and not shunned."*

Still, too many teens—500,000, or one of every 20 girls between the ages of 15 and 19—give birth each year, according to the National Center for Health Statistics.

And still, the pregnancy rate for African-American teen-agers is more than 2½ times higher than that of white teen-age girls—9.2 percent, compared to 3.9 percent. Rates of pregnancy among Hispanic girls have also dropped, from 10.7 to 10.3 percent, although that rate is still too high as well.

Unfair and Unrealistic

But as much as I am for teen-pregnancy prevention, I am against the kind of decision made by the local honor-society chapter in Kentucky. The idea that these girls were any less "moral" because they got pregnant is unfair and unrealistic.

Does that mean all the other honor-society members were chaste and upstanding, or does it mean that many of them were smarter about using birth control?

And why is it that only pregnant girls get vilified for being pregnant? There has only been one immaculate conception. All the others have required a sexual partner.

So why aren't the boys who get the girls pregnant held to some kind of standard?

I doubt that Williamstown's honor society—or any other honor society—has a rule that says that young men who get young women pregnant are not eligible to become members of local honor-society chapters.

I think any teen-ager, especially a pregnant one, who can maintain honor-society-level grades should be applauded and not shunned. In fact, educational institutions ought to be doing everything they can to make sure that pregnant teens stay in school—and finish school.

Armed with an education, the chances are less that they will end up in poverty—which is the plight of so many children born to single mothers.

The teen-ager who is close to my heart is a strong girl. She will fight as hard as she can to stay in school.

I know I'll be cheering her on—to join the honor society or attain whatever goal she chooses.

Go, girl.

Society Should Condemn Teenage Childbearing

by David Popenoe

About the author: *David Popenoe is a professor of sociology at Rutgers University.*

Throughout the history of the world, until the modern era, teen pregnancies were the norm. When a young girl became sexually mature she was married off and soon accomplished that for which she is biologically designed: giving birth to the next generation. Teen pregnancies are still the norm in much of the developing world. Each child born to a young girl normally is considered a blessing.

Not a Blessing but a Curse

But in the developed nations the situation is different. The networks to help the teen mothers—composed of grandmothers; large, extended families; intimate neighborhoods; and working fathers—are seldom in existence. More importantly, women are expected to become educated and, for many, have secure employment before they bear children. Education is considered to be a necessity for living in a complex, information-rich society, and young women today are involved in the work force at about the same rate as young men.

Under modern conditions, teen pregnancies are considered not a blessing but a curse. This is so because most of the children of these pregnancies will grow up fatherless and at high risk themselves for various social and behavioral problems, the education and work lives of their mothers will be seriously impaired, and the welfare and social costs to the nation will be great.

With its very high teen pregnancy rate the United States is seriously out of line with other developed nations. Each year in this country almost one million teenagers become pregnant and approximately four in ten girls become pregnant at least once before reaching the age of twenty. This is twice the rate found in the next highest nation, Great Britain, and nearly ten times the rates found in Japan and the Netherlands. Although the teen pregnancy rate in the United States has dropped some in the past few years, it is still substantially higher

Congressional testimony given by David Popenoe, July 16, 1998.

than in the early 1970s and the drop should not deflect us from grappling with this urgent national problem. Indeed, with many so-called baby boom echo children now entering their teenage years, the total number of teen pregnancies is expected to increase significantly over the next decade.

Perhaps the most alarming trend associated with teen pregnancy concerns the decline of marriage. In 1960, a time of marriage at younger ages and more restricted sexuality, the percentage of unmarried teen births was only 15%. Since then, the increase in out-of-wedlock births has been staggering. Today, some 80% of teen pregnancies and 75% of teen births are to unmarried girls. These girls typically lack the maturity, the skills, and the assistance that are necessary for good parenting.

Sexually Permissive Attitudes

There is a straightforward reason why the unmarried teen pregnancy rate has increased so dramatically—teens are having more sex, at earlier ages, and without the use of contraceptives. In 1970, 35% of girls and 55% of boys reported having had sex by age eighteen. By 1988, the figures were 56% for girls and 73% for boys. Today, if the data were available, the amount of teen sexual activity undoubtedly would be still higher. This is despite a slight decline over the past few years, reported by some studies, in the stated acceptance of casual sex by young people.

One reason for the increase in teen sexual activity is that the age of puberty slowly has been dropping. But the principal reason, in my opinion, is a dramatic increase in sexually permissive attitudes among the young. In a *Wall Street Journal* poll, for example, 47% of respondents ages 18–29 said that "premarital sex is not wrong at all," compared to only 12% of people in the 65 and over age category. Contraceptive use has increased, but the use is often inconsistent and in any event is not enough to offset the increase in sexual activity.

Data about the social consequences of teen pregnancies portray an alarming picture. Less than one-third of teens who begin families before age eighteen ever complete high school; the great majority remain single mothers without fathers to help; and half of all teen mothers and three quarters of unmarried teen mothers end up on welfare within five years of the birth of their first child. As a pathway to a successful life for teenage girls, this is certainly far from desirable.

> *"One of the most important factors in retarding teen sexuality and pregnancies is the disapprobation of society."*

Even more troubling are the negative effects of teen pregnancies on the children involved. These children are far more likely to grow up in poverty, to have more health problems, to suffer from higher rates of abuse and neglect, to fail in school, to become teen mothers, to commit delinquent acts and adult crimes, and to incur failed adult marriages and other relationships. All of this comes at considerable extra cost to the nation's taxpayers. According to one study, which controlled for other differences between teen mothers and mothers aged 20 or 21, teen childbearing costs the taxpayers $6.9 billion each year, or $2,831 a year per teen mother.

A National Moral Decline

The great majority of Americans believe that teen pregnancies are a serious national problem, indeed a problem that is the major component of what is thought to be national moral decline. There is less agreement however, on what we as a nation should do about it. The options range from reestablishing cultural norms, such as a strict moral ban on sexual intercourse before marriage, to comprehensive sex education in our schools, to improving the life options of disadvantaged young people, to the practice of "safe sex" through the placing of contraceptives in the purses and wallets of every teenager.

There is growing agreement within the research community that one of the most important factors in retarding teen sexuality and pregnancies is the disapprobation of society, especially of one's family and peers. A large-scale study funded by the National Institute of Child Health and Human Development for example, found, not surprisingly, that parents' attitudes and relationships with their teen children could be highly influential. The study concluded: "parents who give clear messages about delaying sex have children who are less likely to have early intercourse."

Fundamentally, in my opinion, we need to reestablish across America the simple moral code that young people should wait until adulthood, if not marriage, before beginning a sexually active life. This normally means through adolescence and high school, at least until age eighteen. We must come to the realization that the teenage years in modern times should be for learning and maturing and becoming fully civilized, not for sexuality, pregnancy and parenthood.

In the sense that this norm stands against the powerful thrust of the sexual revolution, and that teenage sexuality seems impossible to curtail, this proposition may appear naive to some. Actually, it has strong support not only among religious bodies but also among parents and teachers and even among teenagers themselves. In one survey, commissioned by *USA Weekend*, seven in ten adults and teens nationwide agreed with "the teen abstinence message." And respondents to a telephone survey of 503 teenagers in grades 9 through 12, when asked their opinion about the right age to start having sexual intercourse, on average said 18 years.

More than 2000 years ago Plato understood that, in the end, there is only one fundamental political issue—how we raise our children. Today, this observation is surely no less true.

The Lives of Teen Parents Are Difficult

by William Plummer and Curtis Rist

About the authors: *William Plummer and Curtis Rist are reporters for* People Weekly.

In 1994, Becky Anderson's room was a typical teenage lair with jewelry, barrettes, tapes and CDs piled on her bed and bureau. In 1995, with a crib and a Swyngomatic and baby toys strewn on the floor, it looks more like a nursery—which it is. Still, the change in Becky Anderson's room pales next to the transformation in Anderson herself since she gave birth to her son Tyler, now 9 months old. "On my birthday, I didn't feel like I'd turned 17," she says. "I felt like I'd turned 30."

Tyler Anderson is one of more than 500,000 babies born in 1995 to teenage mothers—girls who are themselves still in the process of growing up. In 1994, as experts and policymakers debated welfare reform and improving sex education, a team of *People Weekly* reporters and photographers met with teen parents and parents-to-be across the nation. In a cover story on October 24, 1994, many of the teenagers voiced a mixture of regret and optimism, together with an overwhelming resolve to succeed in their new roles.

In the face of so many statistics predicting failure, have they succeeded? In the fall of 1995 we revisited Anderson and most of the other teens in our original story to find out how they are surviving teenage parenthood. "I knew it was going to be hard—and knew it was going to be harder than I thought—but it's even harder than that," says Anderson.

Baby Makes Three

"I kind of miss going out and doing stuff right when I want to," says Amy Smith. "But having a baby kind of makes you feel you're not a teenager anymore, like you don't fit in."

On December 16, 1994, Smith, who turned 18 in October of 1995, gave birth to daughter Amanda by cesarean section. Still living with her mother, she returned to her junior year in high school in Spring, Texas, the following month. But teen life as she had known it had come to an end. In August of 1995 she and Amanda moved to Clinton, Oklahoma, to be with the baby's father, Carmen Arriaga, 21. Though not married—something Smith calls too big of a step— they have established something rare among teenage parents: a nuclear family.

The couple pay rent and share expenses for the small, three-bedroom house they live in with Arriaga's sister and brother-in-law. After a 12-hour shift spent working for $8.42 an hour on a production line making carpeting for cars, Arriaga can't wait to see his daughter. "The best part of the day is when I come home," says Arriaga. "I'll walk in, and Amanda will be smiling."

As for the baby's future, Amanda can be "whatever she wants to be," says Smith, who says she doesn't want to be a "pushy parent." For her own future, she hopes to resume high school, then go on to community college. That path is difficult with a baby, she now knows, and she wishes she could have "been a little wiser in everything—in school, in my education. When I had a baby, I had to grow up real fast."

That Trapped Feeling

Seated in the backyard of her sister's house in Rosemead, California, Angela Myada finds little respite from parenting even as her twins, Mandisa and Maresha, take a nap inside. "It's the stress," she says, ticking off a list of worries that have worn her down since the girls were born. . . . The two have constant fights and colds, and it hasn't helped that Myada, 19, has been shuttling them between motels and relatives in an exhausting search for a place to live.

"I love my babies, but I always wish I'd gotten an abortion or never got pregnant," says Myada, who receives no financial support from the girls' father, Lee Franklin, 20, though he does provide an occasional gift—such as a recent pair of matching outfits. Her welfare benefits of $607, plus $167 in food stamps each month, never seem to stretch far enough. The rent alone for her last apartment, from which she was evicted, came to $600.

But Myada may have found a way to break the cycle. She recently moved with her children into the Women's Care Cottage in North Hollywood, a privately owned shelter, and thinks she has found a job house-sitting for an elderly woman. That would give her a $300 weekly salary and a schedule that would let her take a college class or two during the day. A month ago, Myada said, her life "just looked hopeless," but now she sees a chance for change. "It's late at night when I get to my weakest moment," she says. "But then I rest, and it's a new day."

> *"I knew it was going to be hard—and knew it was going to be harder than I thought— but it's even harder than that."*

Becky Anderson knew she shouldn't make too much of it. Still, she was heartened when the 17-year-old father of her newborn son showed up at the hospital in February 1994 for Tyler's delivery. "The next day he passed out cigars to his friends," says Anderson, 17, a high school senior in Evergreen Park, Illinois. "I pictured all three of us going to the zoo, doing stuff together as a family."

Unfortunately, the proud father's interest lasted only slightly longer than the cigars. "It makes me angry that he quit coming around," says Anderson. "I want to hit him."

For the most part, though, she wastes little energy on anger. She needs all she's got for her hectic life. Anderson, who lives in a four-bedroom house with her mother, Debra Tully, her stepfather and two stepsiblings, starts her weekdays at 6:45 A.M. After feeding Tyler, she heads for Evergreen Park High School. Returning home after 3, she plays with her baby (who is cared for during the day by Debra) until 5:30. Then, three days a week, she heads to the local Kmart, where she works as a cashier until 10:30. Then she tackles her homework until 1:30 A.M. and tries to get a few hours sleep before starting again.

> *"I love my babies, but I always wish I'd gotten an abortion or never got pregnant."*

The schedule leaves her little time for a social life. "I look at things differently than my friends," says Anderson, who plans to go to Fox College in Oak Lawn, Illinois, and study accounting. "Their lives revolve around partying and drinking. To me, work is serious. I can't goof off. I have Tyler—I have to make a better life for him."

A Willing Father

"I was happy with the two kids we got," says Jeffery Mims, 21, sitting in the simply furnished New York City housing project apartment that he shares with girlfriend Twanna Gaines, 18, and their son and daughter. "But I thought about it. There wasn't no alternatives."

At a time when many couples would find themselves stressed by the presence of one child, Mims and his girlfriend are expecting a third. The baby, due in January 1995, is bound to strain their resources, but so far Mims has proved equal to the challenge. "I was real angry at first," says Mims, who said the couple briefly considered an abortion. "We'll work in this one, but this is it."

When Mims fell in love with Gaines, she was already pregnant by another man, but Mims promised to stick by her. And, unlike most of the young men interviewed for our story, he has reared little Jeff, now 3, as if he were his own. Their daughter Jac'Quazia is 20 months old.

Jeff's boss, Michael Friedman, president of a New York publishing house that produces books on gardening and interior design, says Mims "has really gotten a sense of responsibility" in his job as an office clerk over the last two years. Recently, Friedman gave him an unexpected hug, told him he wanted him to succeed, and offered him additional computer work in the business division. "It was shocking," says Mims. "He's focusing on my future. He took an interest in me."

Out of Her Class

Colleen Fitzgibbons, 17, stifles a yawn as her earth-science teacher at Lakewood High School, near Denver, discusses how shale metamorphoses into slate. It's only a little past 1 P.M., but for Fitzgibbons, who has been up since 5:45, it has already been a long day. She is the only mother and senior in this freshman class, a course she failed three years ago, before her own metamorphosis. Fitzgibbons has matured. "Before, I would never have repeated earth science even though I needed it," she says.

In February 1995, Fitzgibbons gave birth to daughter Alexis, whose toys now mingle with her mother's collection of stuffed animals in a basement bedroom of Colleen's parents' house. Though Fitzgibbons works one night a week as a waitress at the local Elks Lodge, her parents pay most of her expenses—including her $100-a-week babysitting bill. "I can't buy things for Alexis myself, and that makes me feel bad," says a teary-eyed Fitzgibbons, who plans to go to college so that she can eventually support her daughter.

Two months ago, Fitzgibbons split up with Alexis's father, Lenny Armenta, a telephone company employee. While they work out their finances, he has agreed to care for the baby three nights a week. "It's a lot harder than I expected," says Armenta, 19, his attention divided between Alexis and a televised football game in his parents' living room. "They go to the bathroom a little more than you expect."

Motherhood Is for Grown-Ups

Motherhood is for grown-ups, and Tori Michel's mother isn't going to let her forget it. When Michel, 18, graduated from high school in May 1994, friends and relatives helped her celebrate with checks totaling $300. For a moment, Michel imagined spending the money like a teenager—toward a down payment on her first car.

No such luck. Michel, who gave birth to daughter Caitlin in September 1994, lives in suburban St. Louis with her mother, Susan, who decided that the windfall should go toward daily expenses, including rent. "I was mad," says Michel. "That was my money! After 13 years of school!" Susan didn't waiver. Tori Michel may not have understood the cost of raising a child before, she says, but "it's getting realer to her."

Lessons in Reality

Money continues to be Michel's biggest concern. "If you've got problems with money, you get crabby. You end up taking it out on everybody, including her," she says, nodding toward Caitlin. The baby's father, whom she met on "a one-night thing," gives her nothing. "I don't think he gives a rat's butt," says

Chapter 5

Michel. Food, diapers and rent swallow up the $446 she receives in benefits, but still she longs for independence from her mother.

With a $650 loan from her divorced parents, Michel began classes recently at St. Charles County Community College and hopes one day to become a counselor—perhaps helping troubled teens navigate "stuff like I have been through." She credits Caitlin with giving her the motivation to continue through school. "Before I had her," Michel says, cuddling her daughter, "I was on a one-way ticket to nowhere."

Unwed Teen Mothers Are Not Academic Role Models

by Kay S. Hymowitz

About the author: *Kay S. Hymowitz is a contributing editor of* City Journal.

In 1990 the National Office of Education Statistics produced some astounding poll results. When 10th-graders were asked whether they would consider having a child without being married, only 53% said no. The remaining 47% said either they would or they weren't sure.

Marriage Is an Option

These results should be emblazoned in everyone's mind now that, in 1998, two Kentucky high school juniors are suing their school board for denying them entrance into the National Honor Society apparently because they are unwed mothers. The two 17-year-olds, Somer Chipman and (yes, really) Chasity Glass, merely reflect the shrugging attitude toward marriage shared by almost half of their peers.

It's hardly the kids' fault. Adults have taught them that rearing children within marriage is merely one of life's varied options. Nationwide, the out-of-wedlock birthrate stands at over 32%; in some areas, especially in the inner city, the rate is more than double that. Almost every week we read about a celebrity who has chosen to go dadless, with Jodie Foster the most recent example.

In many places, high schools provide day care centers for students' babies. Unmarried teen mothers have been honored as cheerleaders, homecoming queens and class presidents. Such efforts may seem compassionate, but they send an unmistakable message that unwed teen childbearing is normal.

A Case of Sex Discrimination?

The American Civil Liberties Union [ACLU], representing Ms. Glass and Ms. Chipman in their suit, argues that this is a case of sex discrimination. According to the ACLU, the girls are being punished for engaging in premarital sex. Since no boy has been disowned by the National Honor Society for having sex— ergo, the girls are victims.

"We are individuals and deserve fair and equal treatment," says Ms. Chipman. Thus one of the country's major social problems turns into a question of individual rights. And a benign slap on the wrist for those who exacerbate that problem becomes an extreme and legally actionable personal affront. Never mind that nobody is talking about kicking the two girls out of school, sending them to Aunt Mary's in Dubuque for six months and then tearing them away from their babies, or, as Sara Mandlebaum of the ACLU accused, making them wear "a scarlet P."

> *"The National Honor Society is right to reject the idea that childrearing within marriage is merely a matter of personal preference."*

Like the ACLU, school authorities appear to have made the defining issue premarital sex rather than out-of-wedlock childbearing. In doing so, they may be giving unwitting support to the prevailing blasé attitude about marriage. "The admissions committee did not feel that someone who had engaged in premarital sex should be held up as a role model," explained Donald J. Ruberg, lawyer for the board of education.

Of course it's true that high school kids shouldn't be having sex—but unwed childbearing is a much graver matter. Emphasizing sex allows unwed young mothers, in time-honored adolescent fashion, to denounce their elders for hypocrisy. "I made a mistake," concedes Ms. Glass. "It's just that others haven't gotten caught." A tellingly childish phrase, "getting caught"—as if becoming pregnant were the equivalent of exceeding the speed limit and being unlucky enough to be seen by a policeman.

Student-Mother as Heroine

Another issue clouds the more fundamental problem of out-of-wedlock childbearing: welfare. If the image of the welfare-dependent teenage mother is the embodiment of the problem, then the high-achieving student-mother becomes a heroine. "Not all teen mothers are stereotypes," Ms. Glass argues. "I want to be a teacher. I didn't drop out of school."

Thus what should be a cautionary tale becomes an inspirational one—a story of an Everyteen who succumbs to sexual temptation. Meeting what Ms. Glass refers to as "the challenge of being a teenage mother," she overcomes great odds and becomes an exemplary student. The language of a *New York Times* editorial captures the spirit exactly: "Ms. Chipman's and Ms. Glass' achievements—doing well in school in spite of their parental responsibilities—prove that an unplanned pregnancy does not have to derail a student's academic career and aspirations. Any honor society chapter should be proud to count them as members."

If, idealistic and hungry for accessible tales of moral courage, many adolescents romanticize their mothering peers, others, deprived of any language of moral seriousness, merely wonder what's the big deal. Ms. Glass has stated her intention of speaking out to her fellow teens about the stresses of unwed mother-hood. But with her blonde, perky good looks, her adorable baby, her high grades and, if she prevails in court, her position in the National Honor Society, Ms. Glass will be no more convincing a poster child for the perils of out-of-wedlock motherhood than will Jodie Foster. She's doing great. What's the problem?

The young have only the moral materials we hand down to them with which to reconstruct the world. The National Honor Society is right to reject the idea that childrearing within marriage is merely a matter of personal preference.

Bibliography

Books

Shirley Arthur
Surviving Teen Pregnancy: Your Choices, Dreams, and Decisions. Buena Park, CA: Morning Glory, 1996.

Robert Coles
The Youngest Parents: Teenage Pregnancy as It Shapes Lives. New York: Norton, 1997.

Paula Edelson
Straight Talk About Teenage Pregnancy. New York: Facts On File, 1999.

Julie Endersbe
Teen Sex: Risks and Consequences. Mankato, MN: LifeMatters, 2000.

Maggie Gallagher
The Case for Marriage. New York: Doubleday, 2000.

Elaine Bell Kaplan
Not Our Kind of Girl: Unraveling the Myths of Teenage Motherhood. Berkeley: University of California Press, 1997.

Michael Lind
Up from Conservatism: Why the Right Is Wrong for America. New York: Free, 1996.

Melissa Ludtke
On Our Own: Unmarried Motherhood in America. Berkeley: University of California Press, 1999.

Kristin Luker
Dubious Conceptions: The Politics of Teenage Pregnancy. Cambridge, MA: Harvard University Press, 1996.

Mike A. Males
The Scapegoat Generation: America's War on Adolescents. Monroe, ME: Common Courage, 1996.

Jane Mauldon and Kristin Luker
Contraception Among America's Teens: The News Is Better than You Think. Berkeley: Graduate School of Public Policy, University of California, 1995.

Rebecca A. Maynard, ed.
Kids Having Kids: Economics, Costs, and Social Consequences of Teen Pregnancy. Washington, DC: Urban Institute, 1996.

Barbara Miller
Teen Pregnancy and Poverty: The Economic Realities. New York: Rosen, 1997.

Mary Pipher
Reviving Ophelia: Saving the Selves of Adolescent Girls. New York: Ballantine Books, 1995.

Laurie E. Rozakis
Teen Pregnancy: Why Are Kids Having Babies? New York: Twenty-First Century Books, 1995.

Sharon Thompson   *Going All the Way: Teenage Girls' Tales of Sex, Romance, and Pregnancy*. New York: Hill and Wang, 1995.

Periodicals

Mary Abowd   "What Are Your Kids Learning About Sex?" *U.S. Catholic*, April 1996.

Jane Brody   "Parents Can Bolster Girls' Fragile Self-Esteem," *New York Times*, November 11, 1997.

James Brooke   "An Old Law Chastises Pregnant Teen-Agers," *New York Times*, October 28, 1996.

William F. Buckley   "Zounds! Enforcing the Law in Idaho!" *National Review*,
Jr.   August 12, 1996.

Suzanne Chazin   "Teen Pregnancy: Let's Get Real," *Reader's Digest*, September 1996.

Christianity Today   "Moms Without Marriage," October 25, 1999.

Maggie Gallagher   "The Abolition of Marriage," *Common Sense*, Summer 1996.

Anne Jarrell   "The Face of Teenage Sex Grows Younger," *New York Times*, April 3, 2000.

Tamar Lewin   "Birth Rates for Teen-Agers Declined Sharply in the '90s," *New York Times*, May 1, 1998.

Jane Mauldon and   "Does Liberalism Cause Sex?" *American Prospect*, Winter
Kristin Luker   1996.

Marci McDonald   "Voluntary Community Service," *U.S. News & World Report*, January 5, 1998.

Kim Phillips   "Taking the Heat Off Teen Moms," *In These Times*, March 4, 1996.

Linda Richardson   "Condoms in School Said Not to Affect Teen-Age Sex Rate," *New York Times*, September 30, 1997.

Amanda Ripley   "Stay at Home Moms," *Washington Monthly*, September 1996.

S. Rodenbaugh   "Better Dead than Unwed? Straight Talk on the Stigma of Illegitimacy," *Utne Reader*, May 1995.

Jeannie I. Rosoff   "Helping Teenagers Avoid Negative Consequences of Sexual Activity," *USA Today Magazine*, May 1, 1996.

Wendy Shalit   "Youth Wants to Know: But What Are the Young Women's Magazines Telling Them?" *Wall Street Journal*, March 26, 1999.

Ron Stodghill   "Where'd You Learn That?" *Time*, June 15, 1998.

Kathleen Sylvester   "Preventable Calamity: How to Reduce Teenage Pregnancy," *USA Today*, March 1997.

Gary Thomas   "Where True Love Waits," *Christianity Today*, March 1, 1999.

James Q. Wilson   "No More Home Alone," *Policy Review*, March/April 1996.

Organizations to Contact

The editors have compiled the following list of organizations concerned with the issues debated in this book. The descriptions are derived from materials provided by the organizations. All have publications or information available for interested readers. The list was compiled on the date of publication of the present volume; names, addresses, phone and fax numbers, and e-mail and website addresses may change. Be aware that many organizations take several weeks or longer to respond to inquiries, so allow as much time as possible.

Advocates for Youth
1025 Vermont Ave. NW, Suite 200, Washington, DC 20005
(202) 347-5700 • fax: (202) 347-2263
e-mail: Info@advocatesforyouth.org • website: www.advocatesforyouth.org

Formerly the Center for Population Options, Advocates for Youth is the only national organization focusing solely on pregnancy and HIV prevention among young people. It provides information, education, and advocacy to youth-serving agencies and professionals, policymakers, and the media. Among the organization's numerous publications are the brochures "Advice from Teens on Buying Condoms" and "Spread the Word—Not the Virus" and the pamphlet *How to Prevent Date Rape: Teen Tips.*

Alan Guttmacher Institute
120 Wall St., New York, NY 10005
(212) 248-1111 • fax: (212) 248-1951
e-mail: info@agi-usa.org • website: www.agi-usa.org

The institute works to protect and expand the reproductive choices of all women and men. It strives to ensure people's access to the information and services they need to exercise their rights and responsibilities concerning sexual activity, reproduction, and family planning. Among the institute's publications are the books *Teenage Pregnancy in Industrialized Countries* and *Today's Adolescents, Tomorrow's Parents: A Portrait of the Americas* and the report "Sex and America's Teenagers."

Child Trends, Inc. (CT)
4301 Connecticut Ave. NW, Suite 100, Washington, DC 20008
(202) 362-5580 • fax: (202) 362-5533
website: www.childtrends.org

CT works to provide accurate statistical and research information regarding children and their families in the United States and to educate the American public on the ways existing social trends—such as the increasing rate of teenage pregnancy—affect children. In addition to the annual newsletter *Facts at a Glance*, which presents the latest data on teen pregnancy rates for every state, CT also publishes the papers "Next Steps and Best Bets: Approaches to Preventing Adolescent Childbearing" and "Welfare and Adolescent Sex: The Effects of Family History, Benefit Levels, and Community Context."

Concerned Women for America (CWA)
1015 15th St. NW, Suite 1100, Washington, DC 20005
(202) 488-7000 • fax: (202) 488-0806
website: www.cwfa.org

CWA's purpose is to preserve, protect, and promote traditional Judeo-Christian values through education, legislative action, and other activities. It is concerned with creating an environment that is conducive to building strong families and raising healthy children. CWA publishes the monthly *Family Voice*, which periodically addresses issues such as abortion and promoting sexual abstinence in schools.

Family Research Council
801 G St. NW, Washington, DC 20001
(202) 393-2100 • fax: (202) 393-2134
website: www.frc.org

The council seeks to promote and protect the interests of the traditional family. It focuses on issues such as parental autonomy and responsibility, community support for single parents, and adolescent pregnancy. Among the council's numerous publications are the papers "Revolt of the Virgins," "Abstinence: The New Sexual Revolution," and "Abstinence Programs Show Promise in Reducing Sexual Activity and Pregnancy Among Teens."

Family Resource Coalition (FRC)
200 S. Michigan Ave., 16th Floor, Chicago, IL 60604
(312) 341-0900 • fax: (312) 341-9361

The FRC is a national consulting and advocacy organization that seeks to strengthen and empower families and communities so they can foster the optimal development of children, teenagers, and adult family members. The FRC publishes the bimonthly newsletter *Connection*, the report "Family Involvement in Adolescent Pregnancy and Parenting Programs," and the fact sheet "Family Support Programs and Teen Parents."

Focus on the Family
8605 Explorer Dr., Colorado Springs, CO 80920
(719) 531-5181 • fax: (719) 531-3424
website: www.family.org

Focus on the Family is a Christian organization dedicated to preserving and strengthening the traditional family. It believes that the breakdown of the traditional family is in part linked to increases in teen pregnancy, and so it conducts research on the ethics of condom use and the effectiveness of safe-sex education programs in schools. The organization publishes the video "Sex, Lies, and the Truth," which discusses the issue of teen sexuality and abstinence, as well as *Brio*, a monthly magazine for teenage girls.

Girls, Inc.
30 E. 33rd St., New York, NY 10016-5394
(212) 689-3700 • fax: (212) 683-1253

Girls, Inc. is an organization for girls aged six to eighteen that works to create an environment in which girls can learn and grow to their full potential. It conducts daily programs in career and life planning, health and sexuality, and leadership and communication. Girls, Inc. publishes the newsletter *Girls Ink* six times a year, which provides information of interest to young girls and women, including information on teen pregnancy.

Heritage Foundation
214 Massachusetts Ave. NE, Washington, DC 20002
(202) 546-4400 • fax: (202) 546-0904
website: www.nhf.org

The Heritage Foundation is a public policy research institute that supports the ideas of limited government and the free-market system. It promotes the view that the welfare system has contributed to the problems of illegitimacy and teenage pregnancy. Among the foundation's numerous publications is its Backgrounder series, which includes "Liberal Welfare Programs: What the Data Show on Programs for Teenage Mothers," the paper "Rising Illegitimacy: America's Social Catastrophe," and the bulletin "How Congress Can Protect the Rights of Parents to Raise Their Children."

Manhattan Institute
52 Vanderbilt Ave., New York, NY 10017
(212) 599-7000 • fax:(212) 599-3494
e-mail: info@manhattan-institute.org • website: www.manhattan-institute.org

The institute is a nonpartisan research organization that seeks to educate scholars, government officials, and the public on the economy and how government programs affect it. It publishes the quarterly magazine *City Journal* and the article "The Teen Mommy Track."

National Campaign to Prevent Teen Pregnancy
1776 Massachusetts Ave. NW, Suite 200, Washington, DC 20036
(202) 478-8500
website: www.teenpregnancy.org

The goal of the National Campaign to Prevent Teen Pregnancy is to prevent teen pregnancy by supporting values and stimulating actions that are consistent with a pregnancy-free adolescence. The organization publishes the report "Whatever Happened to Childhood? The Problem of Teen Pregnancy in the United States."

National Organization of Adolescent Pregnancy, Parenting, and Prevention (NOAPP)
1319 F St. NW, Suite 401, Washington, DC 20004
(202) 783-5770 • fax:(202) 783-5775
e-mail: noapp@aol.com

NOAPP promotes comprehensive and coordinated services designed for the prevention and resolution of problems associated with adolescent pregnancy and parenthood. It supports families in setting standards that encourage the healthy development of children through loving, stable relationships. NOAPP publishes the quarterly *NOAPP Network Newsletter* and various fact sheets on teen pregnancy.

Planned Parenthood Federation of America (PPFA)
810 Seventh Ave., New York, NY 10019
(212) 541-7800 • fax:(212) 245-1845
website: www.plannedparenthood.org

PPFA is a national organization that supports people's right to make their own reproductive decisions without governmental interference. In 1989, it developed First Things First, a nationwide adolescent pregnancy prevention program. This program promotes the view that every child has the right to secure an education, attain physical and emotional maturity, and establish life goals before assuming the responsibilities of parenthood. Among PPFA's numerous publications are the booklets *Teen Sex?*, *Facts About Birth Control*, and *How to Talk with Your Teen About the Facts of Life*.

Progressive Policy Institute (PPI)
600 Pennsylvania Ave. SE, Suite 400, Washington, DC 20003
(202) 546-0007
website: www.dlcppi.org

The PPI is a public policy research organization that strives to develop alternatives to the traditional debate between the left and the right. It advocates social policies designed to liberate the poor from poverty and dependence. The institute publishes *Reducing Teenage Pregnancy: A Handbook for Action* and the reports "Second-Chance Homes: Breaking the Cycle of Teen Pregnancy" and "Preventable Calamity: Rolling Back Teen Pregnancy."

Religious Coalition for Reproductive Choice
1025 Vermont Ave. NW, Suite 1130, Washington, DC 20005
(202) 628-7700 • fax:(202) 628-7716
e-mail: info@rcrcorg • website: www.rcrc.org

The coalition works to inform the media and the public that many mainstream religions support reproductive options, including abortion, and oppose anti-abortion violence. It works to mobilize pro-choice religious people to counsel families facing unintended pregnancies. The coalition publishes "The Role of Religious Congregations in Fostering Adolescent Sexual Health," "Abortion: Finding Your Own Truth," and "Considering Abortion? Clarify What You Believe."

Robin Hood Foundation
111 Broadway, 19th Fl., New York, NY 10006
(212) 227-6601 • fax:(212) 227-6698
website: www.robinhood.org

The Robin Hood Foundation makes grants to early childhood, youth, and family-centered programs located in the five boroughs of New York City. It publishes the report "Kids Having Kids: A Robin Hood Foundation Special Report on the Costs of Adolescent Childbearing."

Sexuality Information and Education Council of the U.S. (SIECUS)
130 W. 42nd St., Suite 350, New York, NY 10036-7802
(212) 819-9770 • fax:(212) 819-9776
e-mail: SIECUS@siecus.org • website: www.siecus.org

SIECUS develops, collects, and disseminates information on human sexuality. It promotes comprehensive education about sexuality and advocates the right of individuals to make responsible sexual choices. In addition to providing guidelines for sexuality education for kindergarten through twelfth grades, SIECUS publishes the reports "Facing Facts: Sexual Health for America's Adolescents" and "Teens Talk About Sex: Adolescent Sexuality in the 90s" and the fact sheet "Adolescents and Abstinence."

Teen STAR Program
Natural Family Planning Center of Washington, D.C.
8514 Bradmoor Dr., Bethesda, MD 20817-3810
(301) 897-9323 • fax:(301) 897-9323

Teen STAR (Sexuality Teaching in the context of Adult Responsibility) is geared for early, middle, and late adolescence. Classes are designed to foster understanding of the body and its fertility pattern and to explore the emotional, cognitive, social, and spiritual aspects of human sexuality. Teen STAR publishes a bimonthly newsletter and the paper "Sexual Behavior of Youth: How to Influence It."

Index

Index